The World On Your Doorstep
The teacher, the environment, and integrated studies

McGRAW-HILL series for Teachers

Consulting Editor
Peter Taylor
School of Education, Bristol University

The World On Your Doorstep

The teacher, the environment, and integrated studies

Peter Prosser

Headmaster
Cranborne Middle School
Dorset

McGRAW-HILL Book Company (UK) Limited

London · New York · St Louis · San Francisco · Auckland · Bogotá · Guatemala
Hamburg · Johannesburg · Lisbon · Madrid · Mexico · Montreal · New Delhi
Panama · Paris · San Juan · São Paulo · Singapore · Sydney · Tokyo · Toronto

Published by
McGRAW-HILL Book Company (UK) Limited
MAIDENHEAD · BERKSHIRE · ENGLAND

British Library Cataloguing in Publication Data

Prosser, Peter
  The world on your doorstep: the teacher,
  the environment, and integrated studies.
  —(McGraw-Hill series for teachers)
  1. Local geography—Study and teaching
  (Elementary)—England 2. Local history—
  Study and teaching (Elementary)—England
  3. Conservation of natural resources—
  Study and teaching (Elementary)—England
  I. Title
  372.19   G75

  ISBN 0–07–084132–2

Library of Congress Cataloging in Publication Data

Prosser, Peter.
  The world on your doorstep.
  (McGraw-Hill series for teachers)
  Bibliography: p.
  Includes index,
  1. Teaching.   2. Activity programs in education.
  I. Title.   II. Series.
  LB1027.P87   372.11′02   81–20739

  ISBN 0–07–084132–2   AACR2

0055203

12345 LT 85432

Printed and bound in Great Britain by
Latimer Trend & Company Ltd, Plymouth

374·5745
PRO

116368

Contents

Contents

Preface

The HMI Survey Primary Education in England (HMSO, 1978) criticized the selection and use of subject material in primary schools in the areas of science, geography, and history. It was claimed that frequently such studies remained at a superficial level and did not lead to progression. At the same time, scarce resources are being spent on taking more and more children out of school on day and residential visits to look at their environment at first hand!

The aims of this book are modest. They are, firstly, to help teachers of 7–13 year olds, who feel they may lack specialist skills in science, history, and geography, to achieve some depth of teaching within a practical, integrated framework; and secondly, to suggest ways in which the school, its grounds, and immediate neighbourhood can be used for this purpose, without the expense and problems involved in visits far afield. There is no attempt to prescribe schemes of work; rather, ideas have been discussed in a fairly personal way, so that teachers can think about them and adapt them to their own needs. As far as possible, the approach is free from jargon, and no previous knowledge is assumed. The book seeks to suggest a philosophy and framework for the nonspecialist who sees a study of the environment as an underpinning for the whole curriculum and, therefore, as a truly integrated study rather than a course in 'environmental studies' separate from the rest of the curriculum.

The school's immediate surroundings can provide opportunities for a child's intellectual, emotional, creative, and spiritual development from first-hand experience. Thinking, language, and artistic and musical expression are all linked through a small number of fundamental themes. The ground rules of energy and material exchange, patterns of time and space, are unchanging although life-styles and values are changing all the time.

Chapter 1 derives basic energy patterns from the study of a single, very common plant that can be grown in any odd spot. Chapter 2 moves on to a wider community, and some aesthetic considerations. In Chapter 3 we look at the educational implications of the use of the environment in integrated studies. Chapter 4 considers two restricted sites within the reach of most schools and looks more closely at the idea of adaptation to environment. Chapter 5 develops a large-scale study from local material, namely chalk and flint. Chapters 6, 7, and 8 consider the development of historical concepts and those of time. In Chapter 9 we take a glimpse at the possibilities and development of man-made machines and devices; and Chapter 10 takes us into the wider social community. Chapter 11 concludes with a quick look into the future.

Inevitably, many of the examples chosen for discussion and illustration arise from my own current work with children in a rural middle school. I am conscious that an inner city school would work in a very different way, yet I believe the basic principles are the same, and it is possible, with imagination, to find remarkable opportunities in the most humdrum of sites.

Peter Prosser

Acknowledgements

I should like to pay warm tribute to my friends at Cranborne: colleagues and children in whose company I have spent so many happy hours in the field, and who have taught me so much about their local environment. We have explored together and this book is, by rights, more theirs than mine.

I am most grateful to Clive Daniels for drawing Figs 1.1, 2.5, and 2.6 from photographs, and to the Rev. Robert Prance, Rector of the Quintet Group of Parishes, for kind permission to quote in Chapter 7 from memorials in Cranborne Church and for facsimile, illustrations, and quotations in Chapter 8, Figs 8.1, 8.2, 8.4, and 8.5.

The author and publishers wish to thank the following for permission to reproduce copyright material:

CHAPTER 1: from Thomas Hardy, 'Voices from things growing in a churchyard', in J. Wain (ed.), *Selected Shorter Poems of Thomas Hardy*, Macmillan, London, 1966; Richard McDermott (ed.), 'Colour-Life', in *Spring into Summer*, Wimborne Schools Pyramid.

CHAPTER 2: from Kenneth Grahame, *The Wind in the Willows*, Methuen, London, 1908 and later editions; Richard Jefferies, *The Story of my Heart*, Longmans Green, London, 1883.

1. Change and decay in all around I see . . .

Patterns in the bramble patch

A self-sown bramble patch spills untidily over the broken brick wall where the outside toilets used to be. Nettles, rosebay willowherb, and a stunted elder bush complete the confusion of this neglected corner, which, on sunny September days, buzzes with a variety of insects including many butterflies. Nobody has done anything with it for years. Indeed, because it lay right under people's noses, it achieved a kind of invisibility. This is a pity, because such an unlikely spot contains most of the material for learning the fundamental lessons about the management of our planet!

The original equipment required is simple; something to sit on, a good lens, notebook and pencil, sketchpad, and some time. We start by marking a single shoot covered in ripe blackberries with wool, so that it can be identified again, and watch the insects that come to the fruit. Some of the insects bask in the full sunlight on the leaves; some never seem to alight at all; others descend to feed on the succulent berries. Wasps, for example, tear open the skin with their transverse, biting mouthparts to get at the juicy flesh. The lens brings into focus the purple skin shredding through their jaws, and the astonishing thing is that, provided all our movements are slow and deliberate, we can get close enough to use a lens without disturbing the insects.

Wasps damage the fruit sufficiently for the juice to ooze out, attracting red-eyed, grey-striped flesh flies (Fig. 1.1(a), (b)). These feed in quite a different way; saliva dribbles down a stout proboscis shaped rather like a drain plunger, and up comes a mixture of saliva and partly digested juice. The resulting pulp is sufficiently liquid for butterflies to sip with their delicate, probing proboscises (Fig. 1.1(c)).

These observations suggest a sequence of insect visitors to the fruit. We can see the start of a possible pattern that goes like this:

Blackberry with skin intact
> Wasp tears open skin
>> Flesh fly digests flesh
>>> Butterfly sips liquid only

1

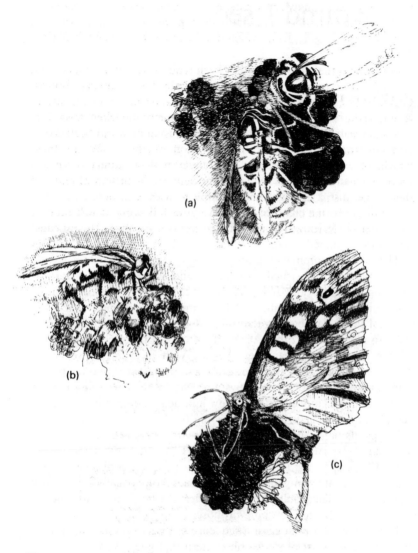

Fig. 1.1 (a) Wasps, (b) flesh fly, and (c) speckled wood butterfly feeding on a blackberry

We can establish whether this *is* a pattern by making repeated observations over, say, fifteen-minute periods and a number of days, the children working singly or in pairs. Recording observations precisely in writing is difficult; modern miniaturized tape recorders make a running commentary possible, from which notes can be constructed later (Fig. 1.2).

In two days the plump berry has been reduced to a dry hulk of skin, through which some of the stones protrude. Other insects abound. Green bottles, midges, hover flies, drone flies, and ichneumon flies are all seen to settle, but not necessarily to feed. Some of the ichneumon flies, for example, will be locating the larvae of flies, moths, and beetles that emerged from eggs originally laid in the flower heads. Within these larvae, they will lay their own eggs and the larvae that emerge will become parasites. Little is known of the detailed life history of many of these insects, still less of their relationships with each other.

Returning to the chain of events we were following, it will become clear that we have only just begun to unravel its links. Unsuspected

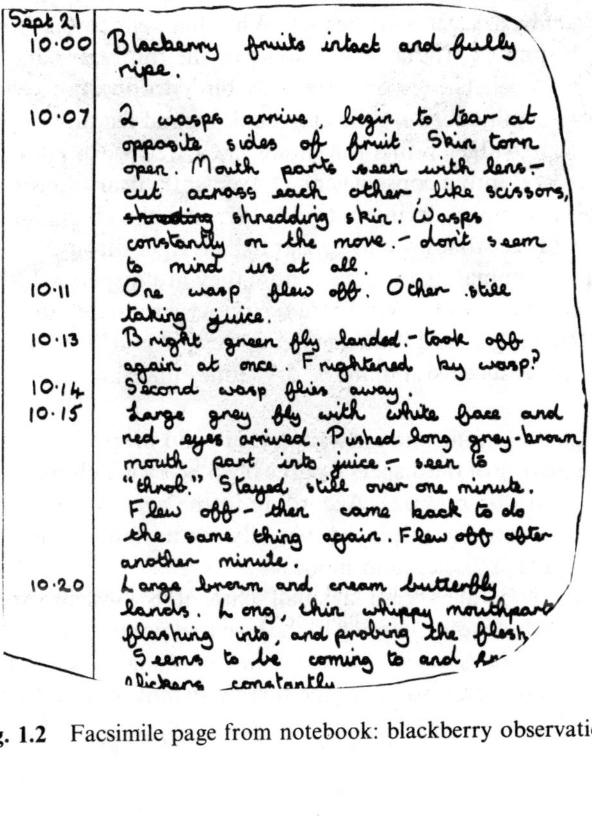

Sept 21

10·00 Blackberry fruits intact and fully ripe.

10·07 2 wasps arrive, begin to tear at opposite sides of fruit. Skin torn open. Mouth parts seen with lens – cut across each other, like scissors, ~~shredding~~ shredding skin. Wasps constantly on the move. – don't seem to mind us at all.

10·11 One wasp flew off. Other still taking juice.

10·13 Bright green fly landed. – took off again at once. Frightened by wasp?

10·14 Second wasp flies away.

10·15 Large grey fly with white face and red eyes arrived. Pushed long grey-brown mouth part into juice – seen to "throb." Stayed still over one minute. Flew off – then came back to do the same thing again. Flew off after another minute.

10·20 Large brown and cream butterfly lands. Long, thin whippy mouthpart flashing into, and probing the flesh. Seems to be coming to and fr[o] flickers constantly

Fig. 1.2 Facsimile page from notebook: blackberry observations armies of spiders hang motionless across their webs; some have trap lines set between their legs like patient fishermen. (Like fishermen, they are quite prepared to cut away the tackle if the catch proves too strong for the line!) The great numbers of spiders gives a clue to the numbers of insects present, for all the spiders are carnivorous. The flesh fly that earlier in the day fed on the blackberry is quite likely to end up as a dry hulk or shell suspended from a web, with all its moist contents sucked into the spider's body.

Spiders, too, have their enemies, for there are small birds just waiting to pick them off; and hiding behind the bricks is the neighbourhood cat, waiting to take *its* toll of the birds.

Here is part of a parody of the rhyme about the House that Jack Built: 'Here lies the cat that ate the thrush that took the spider that caught the fly that sucked up the flesh of the blackberry . . .'. Notice that the rhyme is open ended, and just right for illustration with a flannelgraph or magnet board.

Apart from insects others are interested in feeding on the blackberries. Nearby, the leaves are stained purple with a frothy mess of blackberry stones bound together with mucus. Watching from a little distance reveals blackbirds eating the berries. What happens to the stones? We may see droppings produced, but some of the things are dry, looking very like bird pellets. Are owls the only birds to produce pellets?

Footprints and debris on the clay bank behind lead us to nocturnal feeders. Clear badger prints run alongside a well-worn path, past the allotments, and into a copse where, conveniently near the sett, is a dirt pit full of droppings, drying out and stiff with blackberry stones.

So some of the stones would appear to pass right through the body of a bird or a mammal. Is this, then, how they are dispersed? More and more questions occur. Would the stones germinate after passing through the badger, and if the answer is 'yes', would their germination be more or less successful than the dry stones that fall from the parent plant?

As we go on finding and answering more and more questions, so we build up a picture of the dispersal of the blackberry which comes entirely from our own observations. According to the age of the children the observations can be displayed visually with flannelgraph, charts, overhead transparencies, and models.

We have only uncovered a small part of the blackberry's food relationships, but we are coming to the essential point, that is, *nothing in our whole Universe is static—all is in a state of change.* We can represent the pattern discovered so far in the three different ways shown in Fig. 1.3(a), (b), (c).

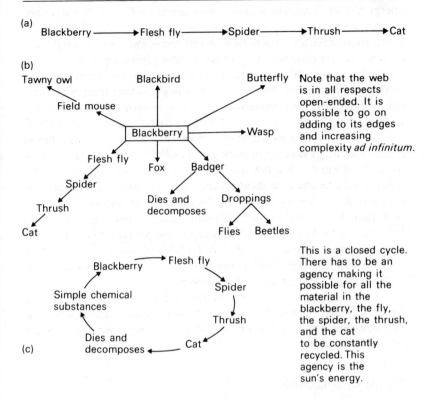

Fig. 1.3 (a) Food chain, (b) food web, (c) food/energy cycle: based on blackberry

Building up and breaking down

Here again, and even more clearly, is the idea that needs to be developed from a very early age, that is, *everything, especially every living organism, is in a state of change, of being built up or of being broken down*. We and every other organism are part of a wonderful, dynamic system of delicate energy relationships, in which the input energy source is the sun and the building materials are a few types—in practice, less than a hundred—but in which the variety of structures is almost limitless. The smallest, normally existing part of each of these units is an *atom*; atoms of the same type make up *elements*; regular combinations of atoms of different types form *compounds*. Carbon, hydrogen, and oxygen are elements. Water and carbon dioxide are compounds; their smallest parts are *molecules*. Water and carbon dioxide come together with the input of

5

energy to form sugars in the process common to all green plants called *photosynthesis.*

Photosynthesis involves building up material, and storing energy. The complementary process of *respiration* involves breaking down, and the release of energy. When the wasp tears open the blackberry skin, the mechanical movements of its body and jaws gain their energy through the burning of food materials in its body (the process we call respiration). The wasp gains a rich, sugary fluid from the blackberry. If the wasp is to survive, its net input of food (holding stored energy) must exceed the energy used up in getting it. Similarly, the spider uses energy in catching the fly. The death of the fly releases material from which other organisms can gain material and energy, as well as the spider. The agents of *decay*, fungi and bacteria, decompose the body of the fly (and of all the other organisms when they die), reducing the complex chains of built-up chemical units to their simple components again (as in a constructional toy like Meccano), and releasing energy. This is where the heat in a compost heap comes from, and this can be studied with thermometers and a pile of lawn-cuttings.

It is obvious that human beings are locked in this closed material/energy cycle without escape. Neither can the planet on which we live escape, for it, too, is part of a finite and very slowly ageing solar system.

Thinking scientifically

By the age of 11 to 13, our children ought to be able to appreciate all the processes and ideas described above, but it is important for the teacher to distinguish between what is true, and what is theory. The words *fact* and *proof* should be used with great care, for what is learned as fact today may well have to be modified tomorrow. This is the history of science. Our observations on the blackberry bush are facts. They are as trustworthy as the observer but the interpretations put upon what we see are speculations, hypotheses, or theories, which need to be sifted and verified. Our blackberry patch provides the means of doing this, too!

Consider the blackberry 'stones'. We can collect those still on the plant in November, those that have fallen on the ground, and we can also collect them from bird pellets and mammal droppings. They all look similarly dead and inert. We can demonstrate that they are not by planting them in soil-pots, and watching them germinate. We can examine the effects of being passed through a bird or mammal, by carefully labelling and segregating the stones, growing them in separate pots under exactly similar conditions of soil, moisture, temperature, etc., so that, as far as possible, the only *variable* is the way the stone was dispersed.

We may put up a *hypothesis* that stones will not die as a result of passing through an animal, since, if this happened, dispersal would not occur. This hypothesis can be tested by carrying out an *experiment* in which this one thing is the variable. We record the results very carefully. The hypothesis may well be true; the gut-travelled stones may germinate, but, from our results, we may suspect something else. Our *new* hypothesis may be that stones germinate more quickly, and in greater numbers (i.e., they are more successful in germination) than those that fall on the ground. Further experiments are needed to see whether this is really so. If it *is* so, how does it happen? What happens to the stone when it passes through the animal? What stops the vital parts from being digested?

So we look carefully at the stones. Older children can take them apart under a low-power microscope, or even find a way of sectioning them. If differences are found in the outer layer of stones, compared with ordinary dry ones, we may put all our *evidence* together, and produce a *theory*, as follows: 'the digestive juices in the gut of the blackbird/badger/fox cause changes which soften the outer layers of the stone so as to allow water to penetrate more readily, and the seed germinates more quickly, than in the dry stones'. This is a *theory*; it fits the available facts better than anything else we can think of, but it is most important to emphasize that we have not *proved* anything!

The kind of investigation we have just looked at applies a scientific way of thinking to a problem. This is *one* of the tools that can be used in studying the world about us, and it was the main point of the Nuffield Junior Science material produced in the early 1960s. The important thing was to provide children with a way of thinking, and of planning action, which would enable them to make a first-hand study of their environment. The body of facts was less important than the way of thinking.

History may well show Nuffield Junior Science to have been a glorious failure, since it did not produce the structured material that teachers were then used to. It concentrated, perhaps too much, on ways of thinking, and at that time most secondary and primary teachers had received all too little training in teaching children to *think* scientifically.

The Schools Council Science 5–13 Project developed materials in a much more structured way, and showed in considerable detail how the scientific thinking of children can be related to their psychological development at different stages. Harlen's (1972) is most helpful for this purpose, and her book should be carefully studied by all who want to work with their children in a first-hand study of their environment, rather than follow someone else's scheme at second hand, or work from books.

Art and literature

In our old 'nature study' classes, we often observed at first hand, collected, drew, described, and sometimes grew and watched plants and animals over stages in their life history. Rarely did we collect much accurate information, and even more rarely did it lead to an experiment as a result of our collective thinking about a problem. What *did* arise from the traditional nature study was an overflow into poetry, art, design, and literature, genuinely integrated in approach, which should never be lost sight of in our passion for scientific thinking. Robin Tanner's work in the 1930–50s is a fine example of what can be achieved aesthetically with children, using their environment as a basis for their work.

We have concentrated in this chapter on scientific thinking. The communication involves language of all kinds, for example, flow charts, tables, oral and written description, drawings, photographs. This concentration on language, transactional and interpretative, is itself a justification for working at first hand, especially with such a limited area as our bramble patch. But it is important to redress the balance since creativity flows readily from the same source. Leaf mosaics, seasonal variations, even a dropped feather, trigger off expressions of a deeper and a broader understanding.

Thomas Hardy, the Dorset poet, knew all about the processes of change. His preoccupation with death is found in much of his poetry, but his awareness of the central concept of this chapter is nowhere more evident than in this poem (see Wain, 1966):

Voices from things growing in a Churchyard

These flowers are I, poor Fanny Hurd,
    Sir or Madam,
A little girl here sepulchured
Once I flit-fluttered like a bird
Above the grass, as now I wave
In daisy shapes above my grave,
    All day cheerily,
    All night eerily!

— I am one Bachelor Bowring, 'Gent', —
    Sir or Madam;
In shingled oak my bones were pent;
Hence more than a hundred years I spent

In my feat of change from a coffin-thrall
To a dancer in green as leaves on a wall,
    All day cheerily,
    All night eerily!

— I, these berries of juice and gloss,
    Sir or Madam,
Am clean forgotten as Thomas Voss;
Thin urned, I have burrowed away from the moss
That covers my sod, and have entered this yew,
And turned to clusters ruddy of view,
    All day cheerily,
    All night eerily!

— The Lady Gertrude, proud, high-bred,
    Sir or Madam,
Am I — this laurel that shades your head;
Into its veins I have stilly sped,
And made them of me; and my leaves now shine,
As did my satins superfine,
    All day cheerily,
    All night eerily!

— I, who as innocent withwind climb,
    Sir or Madam,
Am one Eve Greensleeves, in olden time
Kissed by men from many a clime,
Beneath sun, stars, in blaze, in breeze,
As now by glow-worms and by bees,
    All day cheerily,
    All night eerily!

— I'm old Squiree Audeley Grey, who grew,
    Sir or Madam,
Aweary of life, and in scorn withdrew;
Till anon I clambered up anew
As ivy green, when my ache was stayed,
And in that attire I have longtime gayed
    All day cheerily,
    All night eerily!

— And so these maskers breathe to each,
    Sir or Madam,
Who lingers there, and their lively speech
Affords an interpreter much to teach,
As their murmurous accents seem to come
Thence hither around in a radiant hum,
    All day cheerily,
    All night eerily!

Here is a poem written by an eleven-year-old boy (McDermott, 1979) who had thought deeply about the essential processes of energy and material exchange.

Colour — Life

What colour means life?
Red for blood,
Transporting life—giving oxygen through our bodies,
Green for chlorophyll
In the plants that keep the oxygen going,
Orange, yellow and white for the sun,
That powers the chlorophyll.
Black for oil and coal
Which powers our machinery,
Keeps us warm when the sun is gone.
So is the sun life?
Spring—the return of the sun—is the return
    of life from the depths of winter?
'If spring is life, is it colourful?'
Well might you ask.
Are you by some fault of fate blind?
Look around you; see—
Colour a taste of life!

Enriching the school grounds

There are advantages in working thoroughly over a period of years in the same limited area, and with a small number of plants and animals. For one thing, all kinds of aids to identification can be made; keys, charts, and illustrations.

Many schools, even in town centres, are fortunate in having a neglected, derelict patch which supports a wild or semi-wild community. Piles of stones and logs, leaf mould and soil brought in bags, even sheets of corrugated iron and old cans will develop a population of woodlice, snails, beetles, and centipedes, which can all be brought indoors for a time for study. Seeds and seedlings can be deliberately planted. Fruits and seeds of subjects like bramble and rosebay willowherb can be collected, dried, and germinated in pots, providing a source of material on the school premises, with no expenditure of scarce resources (see Fig. 1.4). Chinnery (1977) is a source of many ideas. Other sources are given in the bibliography at the end of the chapter.

Experimental work can be done on an even smaller scale by keeping very small controlled habitats within the school, or even the classroom. The aquarium is the classical subject, since energy and material balance can be seen so clearly in the relationships between its plants and animals.

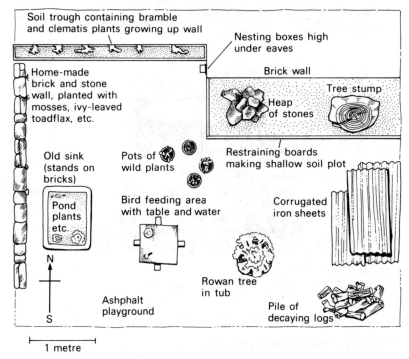

Fig. 1.4 Plan for a wild area in a school playground

Much less often done, but possible, is to keep a small tree stump or rotten log or a section of a limestone wall in school. In town schools, suitable material can be brought in from a weekend excursion by car, and kept for long periods, once the problem of drying up has been overcome. A light wooden frame covered with polyglaze is suitable with a waterproof base or tray covered with a layer of soil, peat, and turf. The moist, rotten stump, complete with mosses, fungi, and other plants can then be installed (Fig. 1.5). Light and moisture can be adjusted. The main interest comes in experimenting with colonization by 'planting' stones of blackberry, elder, and other fruits in crevices where there is a little mould and watching them germinate. A complete woodland scene, with primroses and other flowers, can be encouraged to grow together with an appropriate range of small animals such as spiders and harvestmen. Dated diaries can be kept, and observations made, actually within the controlled environment of the school.

11

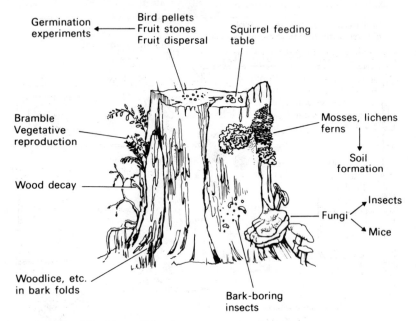

Germination experiments

Bird pellets
Fruit stones
Fruit dispersal

Squirrel feeding table

Bramble
Vegetative reproduction

Mosses, lichens
ferns

Soil formation

Wood decay

Insects

Fungi

Mice

Woodlice, etc. in bark folds

Bark-boring insects

Fig. 1.5 Lines of development starting from a tree stump

Compost and coal

Returning to our earlier observations on the fate of the atoms and molecules that at a given moment made up our ripe blackberry (or any similar first-hand observations), once the children have grasped the idea that the same set of 'parts' is constantly being recycled, that energy plays a vital part in the processes of building up and breaking down, and that all of the energy originates in the sun, there are other first-hand investigations to be made. Two important ones may be mentioned.

We need soil, for pots, trays, for our experimental plots, for our wild corner. In a town school, it may be necessary to bring in, or make, every scrap of soil. This is where the compost heap comes in. Dead leaves, grass mowings, dead flowers, uncooked vegetable waste, not only provide valuable compost as an end product, but we can insert thermometers and make graphs following the processes of decay, and we can make a frame to *use* the heat of the compost in propagating seedlings. Do they germinate and grow more quickly than those at a lower temperature?

Last, but certainly not least, we can see just what happens to all the material that goes on to the heap, ending up in that desirable crumbly mass that the gardening books say we should have!

Beech and oak leaves from the playground and grass mowings are recycled almost on the spot, but what about the orange peel from Israel, the apple cores from Italy, the banana skin from the Windward Islands? Here is material for another chart, and as food for thought. The lettuces we grow in that compost next year could end up containing atoms from three continents (Fig. 1.6)! What a rich and almost global tapestry of change we are uncovering.

The second investigation concerns coal. When we throw a piece on the fire, do we stop to consider what we are doing? The yellow flames leaping up indicate the release of carbon into the atmosphere, in the form of the gases carbon monoxide and carbon dioxide. This carbon was last free in the atmosphere millions of years ago, when it passed through giant ferns

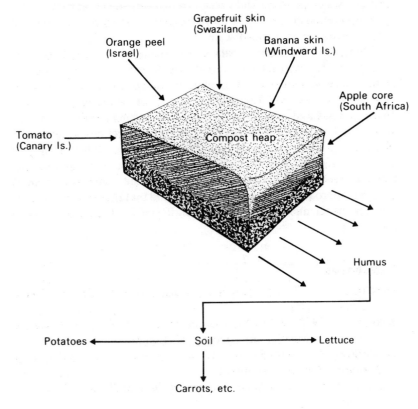

Fig. 1.6 The international compost heap

and horsetails of the warm carboniferous swamps, those whose beautiful fossils we often find in coal shales today.

These carbon atoms have been *dormant* for perhaps 300 million years, until the moment of their release. Now, they are free to circulate again, through lettuces and worms, blackberries and badgers!

Perhaps we could pause to reflect on the carbon atoms locked up in all those millions of tons of coal, oil, and natural gas that have been burned off in the last hundred years. Could they yet be enough to bring about a significant change in the balance between the oxygen and carbon dioxide in the atmosphere?

Summary

We have moved a long way in this chapter, from some apparently trivial observations of insects feeding on blackberries, through the fundamental processes of chemical and energy exchange involved in building up (photosynthesis) and breaking down (respiration) to a consideration of energy dynamics on a world scale.

The implications of energy balance and exchange, the conservation of energy, and the responsible stewardship of our planet's resources are as important in the education of our children (*all* our children) as the skills of reading and writing. The approach need not be complicated if it is based on first-hand observations, and if the thinking required is geared to what is known of the stages of children's intellectual development. Neither does it require a great deal of specialized knowledge on the part of the teacher. But it does need cooperation between teachers so that through their school courses children meet the same fundamental concepts approached in a variety of ways, and that they express them in different media, and go beyond the scientific mode of thinking in doing so.

References

CHINERY, M. (1977) *The Family Naturalist*, MacDonald and Jones, London.

HARLEN, W. (1972) *With Objectives in Mind, Schools Council Science 5–13 Project*, Macdonald Educational, London.

MCDERMOTT, R. (1979) *Spring into Summer*, Anthology produced by Wimborne Schools Pyramid.

WAIN, J. (1966) *Selected Shorter Poems of Thomas Hardy*, Macmillan, London.

Bibliography

ARNOLD, N. (1976) *Wildlife Conservation by Young People*, Ward Lock, London.

ARNOLD, N. (1978) *The Young Naturalists Guide to Conservation*, Ward Lock, London.

DENNIS, E.(ED.), (1972) *Everyman's Nature Reserve, Ideas for Action*, David and Charles, Newton Abbot.

SOPER, T. (1978) *Wildlife Begins at Home*, Pan, London.

TEAGLE, W. G. (1978) *The Endless Village. The Wildlife of Birmingham, Dudley, Sandwell, Walsall and Wolverhampton*, Nature Conservancy Council, London.

WATSON, G. G. (1971) *Fun With Ecology*, Kaye and Ward, London.

2. Down in the ditch

Intense personal experience

Mole thought his happiness was complete, when, as he meandered aimlessly along, suddenly he stood by the edge of a fullfed river. Never in his life had he seen a river before—this sleek, sinuous, full-bodied animal, chasing and chuckling, gripping things with a gurgle, and leaving them with a laugh, to fling itself on fresh playmates that shook themselves free, and were caught, and were held again. All was a-shake and a-shiver—glints and gleams and sparkles, rustle and swirl, chatter and bubble. The Mole was bewitched, entranced, fascinated. By the side of the river he trotted as one trots when very small, by the side of a man who holds one spellbound with exciting stories; and when, tired at last, he sat on the bank while the river still chattered on to him, a babbling procession of the best stories in the world, sent from the heart of the earth to be told at last to the insatiable sea . . .

In this first chapter of *The Wind in the Willows* (Graham, 1908 and later editions) Mole suddenly had one of those intense personal experiences, every detail of which can clearly be recalled years later.

A Wiltshire writer (Jefferies, 1883) tells of a similar experience, pouring out his feelings in a remarkable autobiography:

Moving up the sweet, short turf, at every step my heart seemed to obtain a wider horizon of feeling; with every inhalation of rich, pure air, a deeper desire. The very light of the sun was whiter, and more brilliant here. By the time I had reached the summit I had entirely forgotten the petty circumstances and annoyances of existence. I felt myself. There was an intrenchment on the summit, and, going down into the fosse, I walked round it slowly to recover breath. On the South-Western side there was a spot where the outer bank had partially slipped, leaving a gap. There was a view over a broad plane, beautiful with wheat, and enclosed by a perfect amphitheatre of green hills. Through these hills there was a narrow groove or pass southwards, where the white clouds seemed to close in the horizon. Woods hid the scattered hamlets and farmhouses, so that I was quite alone.

I was utterly alone with the sun and the earth. Lying down on the grass, I spoke my soul to the earth, the sun, the air, and the distant seas, far beyond sight. I thought of the Earth's firmness. I let it bear me up; through the grassy couch there came an influence as if I could feel the great earth speaking to me. I thought of the wandering air—its pureness which is its beauty. The air touched me and gave me something of itself. I spoke to the sea; though so far, in my mind I saw it, green at the rim of the earth, and blue in the deeper ocean; I desired to have its strength, its mystery and glory. Then I addressed the sun, desiring the soul equivalent of his light and brilliance, his endurance, and unwearied race. I turned to the blue heaven over, gazing into its depths, inhaling its exquisite colour and sweetness. The rich blue of the unattainable flower of the sky drew my soul beyond all definition; prayer is a puny thing to it, and the word is a rude sign to the feeling, but I know no other . . .

Touching the crumble of earth, the blade of grass, the thyme flower, breathing the earth-encircling air, thinking of the sea and the sky, holding out my hand for the sunbeams to touch it, prone on the sword in token of deep reverence—thus I prayed that I might touch to the unutterable existence, infinitely higher than deity . . .

Not very far away from us is a fosse such as Jefferies describes. We call it 'the ditch'. Its steep sides are often dark and mysterious, but sometimes, if you get there on a raw February morning, just as the sun is pushing through the mist, you can see the dried stalks of last year's hogweed, picked out for a moment in a golden filigree, edged with sparkling frost crystals. The moment quickly passes, and the stalks merge again with their dull, grey background.

In this and later chapters, we shall meet a number of experiences whose appeal is to the emotions, as well as to the intellect. Children vary much in their sensitivity; not all, by any means, are poets. Yet all should have the chance to make fundamental discoveries of 'feeling', like Mole's, to come face to face in a fresh way with the shapes, colours, smells, and sounds of a wilderness, however small and restricted the experience.

The writer Kenneth Alsopp pointed out some years ago the many subtle evidences there are for the fact that deep within even the most unsuspecting city-dweller there exist echoes of his agrarian ancestry. Only rarely do they surface with the passion of a Jefferies, or the grace of a Wordsworth, but their realization adds a dimension to many lives. Hence the enormous popularity of fishing, sailing, bird-watching, fell-walking, camping, and even just getting out into the park for the afternoon. The child with parents and teachers who will go out of their way to provide opportunities for finding and sharing these brief, intense experiences is fortunate indeed.

We somehow assume that 'creative' writing and poetry will pour out of our children, but it will only come from sharing in first-hand experience, and learning to use all the senses—as Richard Jefferies did—to pass from being an observer to being a participant; enthusiasm (especially on the part of the teacher) is the vital ingredient.

Suitable moments have to be seized; the times and places are subtle and unpredictable, involving mood, weather, light and shade, time of day, and many other factors; success comes when you see a child rush to find a piece of paper to get something down before the memory of it fades!

Such work does not fit readily into a school timetable, since it involves many visits to a field site, often in small numbers. Perhaps one of the strongest reasons for taking children away on residential visits is just the chance to go out together, free from a timetable, early in the morning and late at night. Much can be done near home, however, especially if a park or deserted churchyard is nearby.

The ditch

The teacher needs to get to know thoroughly a site near enough to the school to be visited regularly. Our ditch is such a site. The entire system of mounds and ditches is an artificial construction made by man. We can only guess at what it might have looked like in its heydey, two and a half thousand years ago. Probably its chalk sides were scraped clean and gleaming white, topped by tall wooden palisades. Today its slopes are less dramatic and its hollows are mostly filled with hawthorn, blackthorn, and old man's beard.

Over several years, we have studied one short stretch of the ditch in great detail. Its slopes have been placed in their context, using ordnance survey maps and compasses; sections have been made of it by simple survey techniques; the vegetation has been explored through the seasons, and, irrespective of the number of visits made, we nearly always seem to find something new (see Fig. 2.1).

The patterns we saw in the brambles in Chapter 1 were fairly easily revealed there because the number of living things in the system is small. The ditch provides a much more complex system, whose patterns depend on many more factors. So much so that an overall flow diagram would be impossible to produce. A visual presentation *can* be made with drawings, diagrams, and photographs.

Aspect is important; our part of the ditch lies on a north–south axis, so that the western slope receives the early morning sun, and the eastern slope the warmer sun later in the day, but, because of the 45 degree slope, part of the ditch receives direct sunlight for only a very short time. The subsoil is pure chalk, covered with a thin, light soil layer that dries out quickly. Overall is a variable litter of rotten vegetation. First-hand observation is easy; as with the bramble patch, recording the observations is not. Physical measurements vary with the age of the children. Eleven- to thirteen-year-olds can certainly use thermometers to take air and ground readings at different times of day, test the soil for acidity and other properties, dig out, and make a model of a soil profile, find a way of measuring wind strength and direction, and the quantity and effect of

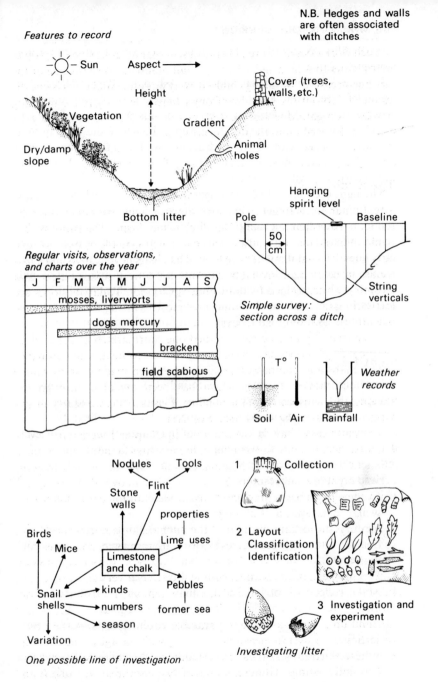

N.B. Hedges and walls are often associated with ditches

Features to record

Sun   Aspect

Height

Cover (trees, walls, etc.)

Vegetation

Gradient

Dry/damp slope

Animal holes

Bottom litter

Hanging spirit level

Pole   Baseline

50 cm

String verticals

Regular visits, observations, and charts over the year

Simple survey: section across a ditch

J	F	M	A	M	J	J	A	S

mosses, liverworts

dogs mercury

bracken

field scabious

T°

Weather records

Soil   Air   Rainfall

Nodules   Tools

Flint

Stone walls

properties

Birds

Lime   uses

Mice

Limestone and chalk

Snail shells   kinds

Pebbles

numbers

former sea

season

Variation

One possible line of investigation

1   Collection

2 Layout
Classification
Identification

3 Investigation and experiment

Investigating litter

Fig. 2.1 Investigating life in a ditch

19

rainfall. All such records, if they can be taken over a number of years, have great value.

In places, tree cover is total, and dense. Ash, oak, elder, and beech give the taller tree cover; hazel, dogwood, privet, white beam and holly provide the shrub layer, and over all spreads a wild carpet of ivy, bramble, and old man's beard. Tree stumps lie where they fall; in time they are colonized with ferns (which also grow almost to the top of some of the living oaks), mosses, and eventually flowering plants like rosebay willowherb and wild strawberry.

The light is comparatively stronger in the winter, when the trees are bare, than in the summer, when the foliage is dense. Mosses, liveworts, and ferns flourish in the dampness of winter and early spring but by the height of summer they are withered. Whatever the season we are surrounded by contrasts of light and shade, gnarled, incredibly old shapes, burgeoning, growing new forms; dog roses bursting out of bud; tiny mosses bearing blood red capsules; spears of light across the bryony berries. In spring you can sit among it and feel it growing; in autumn, you can witness its fading with gentle dignity into the grey of winter.

Identification

Something 'new' is always being found. One of the problems for nonspecialist teachers is how to identify what is found; and one of the common deterrents to working in an open-ended way at field study is an acute awareness of lack of knowledge of the names of things. However, if the teacher is used to working *with* children, drawing and model-making with them, there is no problem; he just identifies with them, too.

Here are a few suggestions:

1. Confine the study to one small area, and get to know its inhabitants well.
2. Identify the organisms that are common, and prepare cards or boards. Older children can do this with drawings, cut-outs, and diagrams.
3. Prepare keys in the ways shown in Figs 2.2 and 2.3.
4. Make collections of labelled nonliving specimens from the study area.
5. Build up a *small* collection of useful identification books (see next section).
6. Where a name is not known, encourage the children to invent a descriptive name. Things were often named in this way originally.

Identification books

The most modern field guides, while they are beautifully produced and illustrated, are not as easy to use as the older ones, since, in order to increase sales, and because people travel widely, they cover Europe and North Africa as well. Many of these newer books are not British in origin. On the other hand, the majority of reference books written for children are not sufficiently detailed. Many of the older books are still obtainable second-hand. The bibliography at the end of the chapter provides two short lists, the first a basic one of useful modern books currently in print, the second, a list of older books to look out for second-hand.

A good identification book covers most of the organisms likely to be seen (but not the unlikely and rare ones), has adequate, simple, coloured pictures, clear short descriptions arranged in a definite order, and probably keys. The RSPB *Guide to British Birds* (Saunders, 1975) is an excellent example of such a book.

Keys

Keys used to be found only in the most advanced identification books. The late nineteenth century was the golden age of key making and many of the keys made then are still in use. Today, even simple books have keys, often visual ones. Organisms are identified by asking a series of questions that are paired to give alternative answers, so you have to have the specimen before you, and examine it carefully, often with a lens. You go on answering the questions, following the correct alternative at each stage, until you reach a positive identification. This is not as easy as it sounds; general keys can be very frustrating. A *home-made local key* is a different proposition. Making keys is in itself an excellent exercise for children. Once made, a key can be duplicated and used from year to year. Fig. 2.2(a) shows a simple key that would apply only to the trees of one particular school's grounds. It was made up by some eleven-year-olds and is based on the shape of the leaves.

Fig. 2.2(b) shows a pictorial layout of the same key, in a form suitable for younger children to use. Other keys can be made to identify the main groups of invertebrate animals (see Fig. 2.3), mosses, and ferns (of which there are not many kinds), and the snail shells (about nine different kinds in our ditch).

As with maps, the keys can be mounted on plywood boards and sealed on both sides with transparent plastic (see Chapter 9). A clip enables the boards to be used as writing and drawing boards as well.

(a)

| Leaves Simple .... 2 | Simple leaves consist of 1 leaflet. |
| Leaves Compound ......1 | Compound leaves have more than 1 leaflet. |

1. *Compound leaves*

Lobes (leaflets) in shape of a hand (palmate). *HORSE CHESTNUT*
Lobes opposite along a straight stalk (pinnate). *ASH*

2. *Simple leaves*

No deep indentations.	*BEECH*
Quite deep indentations.	*OAK*
Indentations drawn out into spikes, upper surface of leaves waxy.	*HOLLY*
Leaf broad, veins carrying lobes like a hand with blunt fingers.	*SYCAMORE*
Leaves just thin spikes, in pairs.	*SCOTS PINE*

(b)

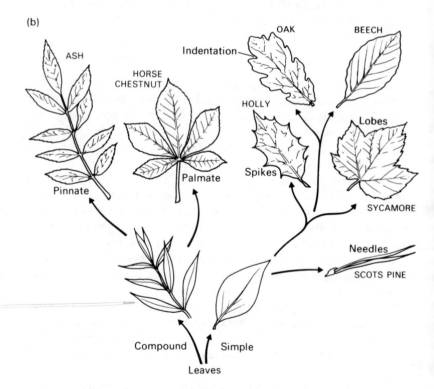

Fig. 2.2 (a) Key to leaves of trees in school grounds. (b) The tree key in diagram form

22

1. Has it got legs? If so, move to 3. If not, move to 2

2. *No legs* (a) Body with a shell   *Snail*

          (b) No shell, long and slimy, sometimes
              with hard pad on back   *Slug*

          (c) Small, white, or almost colourless, body   *Roundworm*
              not divided into segments   (*nematode*)

          (d) Body with segments, one or both ends   *Worm*
Segments   pointed, white, greyish or reddish   (*annelid*)

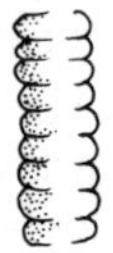

          (e) Body with clear segments, white or grey,
              one end blunt like this:-⊂⟩   *Fly larva*

          (f) Like (e), but with definite black or
              brown head and jaws   *Beetle larva*

          (g) Hard, reddish or brown oval, faintly
              segmented   *Pupa case of fly or beetle*

3. *With legs* (a) Three pairs only, head, thorax and abdomen
              usually seen, may or may not have wings   *Insect*

          (b) More than three pairs

             (i) Four pairs   *Spider or mite* (but see false scorpion)

                  Four pairs long thin legs, oval body   *Harvestman*

             (ii) About seven pairs, body covered
                  in hard plates   *Woodlouse*

             (iii) More than seven pairs
                  One pair legs per segment   *Centipede*
                  Two pairs legs per segment   *Millipede*

This key could be done in a series of drawings, but the
key in the form shown makes it essential for the pupil
to look closely at his/her specimens and gives practice
for the future use of more difficult keys.

Fig. 2.3   Part of a key made by a teacher for class use in identification of small
animals in leaf litter

Collections

Closely connected with identification is the making of collections. The
modern cry is for absolutely *no* collecting, but the collecting instinct goes
deep, especially in children. Certainly at a site repeatedly visited by
groups of children all doing, and looking for, the same thing, there is a
real danger that the visitors themselves are the greatest agent of change.
This is all the more reason for schools quietly to find their own study
sites as near to school as possible, and to develop a sensible pattern of
visiting, so as to affect the local environment as little as possible.

The area around our ditch is visited by many people, throughout the year, but most of them keep to the paths across the top of the mounds, and to the open ground outside them. The inside slopes and bottom of the ditch are almost undisturbed except by our visits.

At least two rare orchids grow on the mounds beside the ditch. Strangely, because one is quite striking, visitors seem to pass by without seeing them. It is, however, necessary to train the children *never* to pick a living plant before drawing the attention of the teacher to it, and only in exceptional circumstances to uproot anything. All animals taken for study should be returned, stones and logs turned to their original positions, and the whole site should bear no traces of our visit when we have gone. This is a matter of *training* from the early years, for the instinct is to *pick*! What, then, can we do with the collecting instinct?

Exploration one damp day with a group of eight-year-old boys yielded the following treasures:

> Pieces of chalk and flint.
> Smooth round or oval pebbles.
> Snail shells of four kinds, some of them damaged in a peculiar way.
> The skull of a small mammal.
> Beech nuts, several having the same kind of interesting incision, and a variety of mosses, and fungi, including the Jew's ear fungus.

Every single one of these objects provided something of interest, and, apart from the plants, could have given rise to a useful and informative permanent collection. In fact, there is a connection between the first four items which could have given rise to the topic mainly developed in Chapter 5.

The removal of objects such as these, in small numbers, does little or no harm, although one can find sites where successive school parties have left a whole wood denuded of everything moveable, while apparently not touching a single living plant.

Straight collections have little value; dated, documented collections all from one area have considerable value. Footprint casts, dried evidence of bird or mammal feeding, e.g., the contents of squirrel feeding tables, bird pellets, bones and skulls, are just a few subjects which could be collected from our ditch. Best of all, is a collection which no one has made before, and for which there is no identification book. Fig. 2.4 shows part of a collection of fruit stones taken from fruits and dried, to provide a known collection of types for working with pellets and droppings.

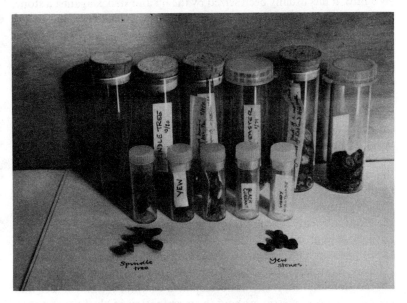

Fig. 2.4 Collection of stones from berries

Detective work

The things we collect often give rise to interesting questions, the answering of which involves considerable detective work. For example, among the beech nuts we found, those with the regular incisions were all empty (infertile nuts); mixed up in the sample were whole, fertile nuts, fertile nuts which had been torn open, and empty nuts with one triangular side torn out. All these forms of damage were clearly the result of some animal's feeding habits. The common animal that came to mind was the grey squirrel, but we had never *seen* one at work on beech nuts. We tried the incisors of several skulls in our collection to see if they fitted the indentations. Fig. 2.5(a), (b) shows that the teeth from a squirrel skull fit the indentations exactly! The full story required considerable observation of the squirrels. The young squirrels (born the previous spring) start tearing open every nut, whether it is full or empty. Since the majority are empty, their frustration is considerable. Their behaviour rapidly becomes modified so that they bite into each nut, spitting it out, if it yields at once. The little scratch marks made by their claws can clearly be seen on the nuts.

The wood snail shell seen in Fig. 2.6 shows a similar problem regarding the damage we can see. Where a shell has been smashed open by a bird, it has usually been seized by the lip and struck against a stone, so that the pieces are quite irregular. The ones we picked up have the top two or three whorls neatly cut out, and the edge shows a row of neat tooth marks—and no living birds have teeth! Reference to a skull collection showed that the incisors of a field mouse matched the serrations almost exactly; afterwards we found confirmation in a book that field mice do indeed include wood snails in their diet. They both come out at night.

Where do we find a collection of small mammal skulls? One answer is to try to obtain some owl pellets, most of which will contain one or more skulls that can be cleaned and mounted suitably. The only problem is that the 'backs of the heads' will have been removed, but since it is the teeth that are mainly required, this will not matter (see Yalden, 1977).

This glimpse of the making and use of collections is far removed from the conventional collections of dried flowers and butterflies. The collections, e.g., of berry stones, and of skulls, are working ones, to be used in answering questions and making investigations.

If we compare the detective work described above with the observations and experiments developed in Chapter 1, it can be seen that in answering our questions about the germination of blackberry stones, we tested our hypothesis by means of controlled experiments, and the

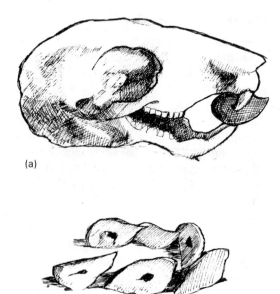

(a)

(b)

Fig. 2.5 (a) Squirrel skull and (b) beech nuts

Fig. 2.6 Wood snail shell damaged by a mouse

evidence for our eventual theory was firm. In addition, we could have gone on refining our experiments to produce more and more exact evidence.

In the case of the beech nuts, and that of the damaged snail shell, we are considering *circumstantial* evidence, the value of which has to be weighed. Until we have actually *seen* the squirrel treating nuts in the way suggested (and eventually we did) we can only put together all the circumstances and see if the explanation fits. In the end, much 'scientific' evidence is circumstantial. It would be impossible for a student to learn all he needs to know at first hand. It is, therefore, all the more important that in his early years, he should learn deliberately to use various modes of thinking in dealing with the problems posed by his environment, to be able to criticize them, and to appraise their use by others. To date, we have not seen a field mouse actually eating a wood snail, even when someone put some snails in a cage with a field mouse one evening, and went to look next morning!

One day there was a light snowfall and we dashed over to the ditch with the camera. There were animal tracks everywhere; we had no idea there was such a population. For the only time, we found clear deer tracks through the bottom of the ditch, having never seen any evidence of deer previously. All kinds of scenes, large and small, caught our eyes that day. Two of the most striking involved a puddle and a twig.

Fig. 2.7 shows the puddle seen looking vertically downwards. Those smooth, curving, symmetrical pressure patterns of ice on a brown background could well be an abstract painting! If it *had* been one, people might have said, 'Yes, very pleasant, but of course, it isn't *real*!'

It did not last long after it had been photographed; a large dog came along and walked straight through it. The twig was a fine example of

Fig. 2.7 Stress patterns on a frozen puddle

'instant art', too. A few horse hairs had rubbed off on the hawthorn twig; droplets of water had frozen on it, so that the crystals dangled gently in a pendant mobile. All too soon, it had melted. The old man's beard was striking, too; but by early afternoon, all had melted and the patterns had gone. We had captured all these moments on coloured slides; we have relived them many times since, and the pictures have been used for drawing, at assembly, and for many other purposes.

We found the puddle and the twig because we *looked*, expecting to see, and our discovery in the ditch that day (the only time we ever saw it covered in snow) could almost rate with Mole's discovery of the River.

The possibilities of the ditch are endless. We could certainly write a book about it. How do you describe the smell of wet moss, or the coming into focus in a lens of leafy liverwort capsules bursting as they dry in the sun, or the sudden glimpse, through a gap, of a kestrel hovering a few feet away against a clear blue sky? We once found nine ladybirds sewn up tight in a white beam leaf, and fourteen roosting common and adonis blue butterflies; the list is almost endless!

You may say that we are particularly favoured in having such a spot, although it looks very ordinary, having been described by one visitor as 'just a dark old ditch', but I found equally ordinary and just as exciting spots in the Bristol parks over six years of working in the city schools.

Mouse hoards, for example, were found to contain monkey nuts; rooks that lived in the park trees were seen to fly inwards to the city, instead of outwards to the grain fields. A nice piece of deduction showed that they were going into a brewery wharf near the docks to feed on the spilled barley (Fig. 2.8). Their pellets even contained little pieces of red brick, probably from a demolition site next door.

A town park rookery, such as the one used here, provides opportunities for studies of many kinds. The deductive study mentioned introduces a considerable range of skills. Studies in communication can be done by synchronizing the use of a tape recorder, a stop watch and a notebook to connect sounds and movement with particular activities. One town school has recently started a study on the modification of rook behaviour brought about by the recent change from cooked school meals eaten indoors to wholesale sandwiches, some of which are eaten in the playground! (In King (1980) the fortunes of a rookery are followed and attractively presented in words and pictures through the months of the year.)

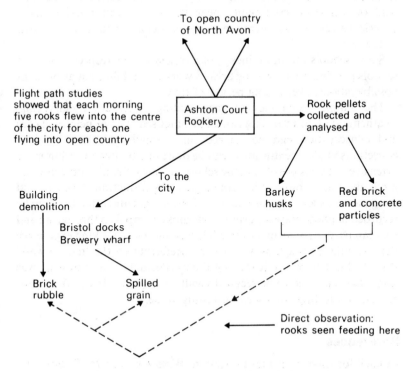

Fig. 2.8 Rook feeding: a deductive study made in a Bristol park

It must be admitted that in our big cities, especially in some areas of postwar development, the wild and green aspect of the environment has been neglected, and even play areas are totally inadequate. Experiences of the kind described in this chapter must have a hollow ring to many teachers in schools in such areas! Even the building materials are now, in many cases, synthetic. It has been argued that to take children out of such an environment for a day, or on a short residential visit, has little value since the influence of it would be so slight when set against their overall experience. Intellectually, there might be little gain, since much of what is seen and done could be brought to the children in one form or another, but, with careful planning, small groups, and sympathetic teachers, the emotional and creative experiences can live with the child all his or her life.

Summary

The first-hand education of the *whole* child is a partnership between the child and the teacher, involving feelings, as well as intellect. A suitable wild or semi-wild community near the school can provide many experiences, especially where a sensitive teacher has made repeated visits to the site.

Some schools are more lucky than others in this respect, but most schools *can* find an interesting area to work at, and find out as much as possible about, over a long period of time.

The simple techniques of map-reading, orientation, surveying, weather and plant recording can all be practised. The principles of care and conservation can be learned on a small scale, and *working* collections made. Identification can be done in a limited area, but more extensively than is possible in the school grounds. Small problems of all kinds abound, some of which can be solved by deduction. Aesthetic and imaginative experiences should be actively sought and often they can be recorded in photographs. A single, wet moss clump seen through a hand lens can be as significant as a much larger and more striking experience that we might go a long way to see. Referring to the 'nature walk' described in Chapter 3, it was not the intellectual content of what was done that remained to be recalled vividly years later. It was the sights, scents, and feelings that were of lasting value.

References

Council for Environmental Education, *Wasteland Plants: Pictures and Schemes for an Urban Environment*, School of Environmental

Education, Reading University, London Road, Reading, RG1 5AQ.

GRAHAME, K. (1908) *The Wind in the Willows*, Methuen, London.

JEFFERIES, R. (1883) *The Story of My Heart*, Longmans, Green, London.

KING, D. (1980) *Rook*, Beaver Books, Hamlyn, London.

SAUNDERS, D. (1975) *RSPB Guide to British Birds*, Hamlyn, London.

YALDEN, D. W. (1977) *The Identification of Remains in Owl Pellets*, Mammal Society, 62 London Road, Reading, Berkshire.

Bibliography

Annotated short list of identification books

MODERN BOOKS

Series

Blandford Colour Series, Blandford, London. Example: *Woodland Life*, a series including Darlington, A. (1968) *Plant Galls* (only readily available book on plant galls).

Clue Books, Oxford University Press, London. Titles: *Bones, Birds, Flowers, Insects, Trees, Freshwater Animals, Seashore Animals*. (Excellent books based on clear keys.)

Handguide Series, Collins, London. Titles: *Birds, Flowers*, etc.

Jogger Pocket Books, Jogger, California Park, Nine Mile Road, Finchhampstead, Wokingham, Berkshire. Examples: Yewlett, G. *Tracks and Trails of the Woodlands, Wildlife Tracks, Finding the Fox*. (Pocket books, laminated to make pages waterproof.)

Observer's Books, Warne, London. Titles: *Ferns, Mosses and Liverworts, Lichens, Trees, Pondlife*, and the more usual groups.

Spotters Guides, Usborne, London. Titles: *Birds, Fishes, Trees*, etc. Example: Leutsher, A. (1979) *Animal Tracks and Signs*. (Vary, but attractive, reliable, and inexpensive.)

The School Natural Science Society, 2 Bramley Mansions, Berrylands Road, Surbiton, Surrey, KT5 8QU. Pamphlets.

Note Series such as the *Penguin Nature Guides* and the *Collins Guides* are excellent but they cover many plants and animals never seen in this country, and, therefore, can be confusing to children.

Individual books

BANG, P. and DAHLSTROM, P. (1974) *Collins Guide to Animal Tracks and Signs*, Collins, London. (Danish originally but has much useful information.)

EDLIN, H. L. (1978) *The Tree Key*, Warne, London.

LAWRENCE, M. J. and BROWN, R. W. (1973) *Mammals of Britain, Their Tracks, Trails and Signs*, Blandford, London.

SPEAKMAN, F. J. (1962) *Tracks, Trails and Signs*, Bell, London.

Note Seaward, M. R. D. (ed.) (1981) *A Handbook for Naturalists*, Constable, London, has a comprehensive book list and much other condensed reference material.

EARLIER EDITIONS

Series

Collins Guides, Collins, London. Example: McClintock, D. and Fitter, R. S. R. (1956) *Wild Flowers*.

Oxford Pocket Series, Oxford University Press, London. Examples: Sandars, E. (1947) *Bird Book* and *Insect Book for the Pocket*.

The Young Specialist Books, Burke, London. Example: Janus, H. (1965) *Molluscs*.

Wayside and Woodland Series, Warne, London. Example: Southwood, T. R. E. (1963) *Life of the Wayside and Woodland* (good for land snails). (Some of these have been enlarged and are in print in new format but expensive.)

Individual books

DALE, A. (1951) *Patterns of Life*, Heinemann, London. (Has keys to animals as varied as newts and woodlice.)

VEDEL, H. and LANGE, J. (1960) *Trees and Bushes*, Methuen, London. (Has pictorial key.)

Warning

Mammal and bird droppings, and, of course, skulls and bones, may present a health hazard. Suitable precautions should always be taken, including the soaking of material for 24 hours in disinfectant or bleach and the handling of such material with disposable plastic gloves which are available cheaply from chemists.

3. Studying the environment

The scene is a busy market town. Almost unremarked among the crowds of shoppers and holidaymakers, group of children go about their business, identifying shops and distinctive architecture, sketching in the churchyard, and asking questions of passers-by.

Similar groups of children can be found working on upland farms, riversides, forests, nature reserves, zoos, seashores, and their common badge of office is often the clip-board. In favoured areas, they are so common, that, like the furniture, they go unnoticed.

Children study their environment at first hand from their very earliest days. Little children explore their home and school for the purpose. Moving up the junior and into the middle school, visits and expeditions become more ambitious, often involving residence some distance away.

Chapters 1 and 2 have shown how much fundamental study can be based on the school grounds and their immediate surroundings. In these days of reduced staffing and resources, it has become necessary to think very carefully about expeditions at some distance away from school, whether they are day or residential. We need to know exactly *how* each one is to be justified. The case revolves round the answers on either side of an equation, as shown in Fig. 3.1.

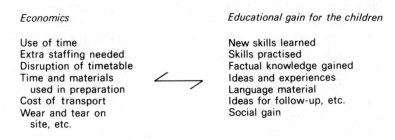

Economics	Educational gain for the children
Use of time	New skills learned
Extra staffing needed	Skills practised
Disruption of timetable	Factual knowledge gained
Time and materials used in preparation	Ideas and experiences
	Language material
Cost of transport	Ideas for follow-up, etc.
Wear and tear on site, etc.	Social gain

Fig. 3.1   Resources/educational gain equation

This book has been written in the belief that a forward looking education, based almost entirely on the environment near at hand, can be developed by teachers who have had no specialist training.

The meaning of environmental study

The purpose of environmental study is to learn through every possible medium about the earth and all that is on it, particularly as it relates to our own surroundings and relationships. It is approached in many ways, involves facts, values, interpretations, feelings and actions, and needs contributions from the thinking of several disciplines. It has an all-embracing purpose, involving a vast field of study. What we actually do clearly needs to be structured in some way so that our children gain progressive experience appropriate to their age and development, and to make sure that overlaps occur only intentionally. A rationale is needed to cover a child's work and experience over, perhaps, his or her first seven or eight years of schooling. This is a long time, in which attitudes can be fixed for life.

In this book we are building up our experience on four fundamental groups of ideas, namely:

1. The idea of energy and energy-exchange.
2. A child's developing concept of space and distance.
3. A child's developing concept of time.
4. Human relationships with the environment, and with other people.

The list looks prosaic; as succeeding chapters will show, the reality can be as imaginative as the teacher is prepared to make it.

Field studies

When I was a boy at primary school our local field excursions were unstructured and unpremeditated. A spring day would come when dandelions spattered the bank with gold, green fingers appeared on the horse chestnut boughs, and the playground gave off a fragrance of warm asphalt. Spontaneously, our teacher would take us up the lane, across the fields, and down to the pond. Gathering festoons of stitchwort, Jack-by-the-hedge, and primroses, we never gave a thought to the evils of flower picking. Jam jars were stuffed with weed and tadpoles, and nobody told us about the danger of glass jars. We looked, listened, and wrote down nothing.

There was very little in the way of follow-up; a few drawings were provided and references to the simplest of identification books, but certainly no experimental work. Yet, years later, more than a few of us could remember every detail of those excursions, the sights, smells, even the conversations. The time and place were right; the opportunity was seized, and we had clearly had a valuable educational experience. Our teacher was not so much knowledgeable as enthusiastic.

The term 'field studies' is applied to all visits and work outside the classroom, other than to work in libraries and museums. We can equally well do field work in the playground, the park, or the local church.

Importance of basing study on the local environment

Twenty years ago words like 'ecology' and 'environment' were in daily use only among a comparatively few academics and professionals. Nowadays they are used (and frequently misused) as part of the everyday language of newspapers and advertisements. *They have become emotionally loaded words, used to influence opinion,* rather than the definitive terms they started out as. Twenty years ago, too, Friends of the Earth, and the Conservation Society were thought by many to be just refuges for cranks. They have become respectable, even distinguished, and on the day I write this, two more new conservation bodies have come into existence, to join the many organizations that are working away to inform and modify public opinion. The 'environment' and man's relations with it have become news. There is a great deal of environmental activity, and it would be encouraging to believe that, because of this, and because environment-conscious organizations have found a voice, the ordinary citizen of the 1980s has a better understanding than his forbears of the natural rules and the factors that enable all of us to live together on this earth, and therefore a greater care for its stewardship. *I do not believe that this is true at present.*

A great deal of relevant knowledge has been built up, and much of it can be presented in simple, concrete ways to five-to-seven-year-olds, so that they grow up with it. Many schools educate in this way, but it will take much longer than twenty years, even if schools were of one mind about what to do (and they are not), to effect mass changes in attitudes that are rooted in the very depths of human nature. *There is a great danger in believing that such changes are taking place when, in fact, they are not.*

Certainly the various oil crises, threats of global war with sophisticated weapons, even the possibility of global annihilation, localized atmospheric pollution, instant communication, and easy travel have combined to arouse unease and insecurity in individuals and populations. Maybe, too, those beautiful photographs of the whole earth, taken from spacecraft and from the moon in the 1960s, did something to make us aware of the delicacy and fragility of the 'spacecraft' we ride on, and the fact that its resources will not last for ever. At the same time as we are urged to preserve or conserve almost everything from flowers to buildings, an opposite view can be put. Oil has been found under the

New Forest, coal under the Vale of Belvoir, both choice beauty spots that ought to be preserved, unless the view is taken that *all* resources are there to be exploited. The ordinary person needs a basis of fact and the ability to think appropriately in order to come to his own conclusions. So, too, does the politician who has to *make* the decisions.

Yet a recent survey of adults in a fairly rural population showed an almost total lack of understanding of such a concept as that of the energy relationship between *photosynthesis* (in which food is made by green plants, and energy stored) and *respiration* (in which energy is released to do work or produce heat in plants and animals). Knowledge of the origins of fossil fuels proved to be equally vague. A significant number of adults thought that fossil fuels were currently being produced in such a way that new sources would become available to future generations, showing a serious misconception of the time scales, as well as of the processes, involved.

Present evidence suggests that most adults do not have as part of their 'thinking equipment' an understanding of the basic concepts, such as those of energy exchange, although many *think* they have. There is abundant evidence that when long-term fundamental issues conflict with a human community's short-term interests, those short-term interests usually prevail. This is why I believe it is dangerous for us as educationists to assume that environmental education has yet made any *fundamental* changes in the attitudes and life-style expectations of most people. One day it must, if we are to live in harmony with our environment and at peace with our neighbours. *One of the purposes of environmental education up to 12 or 13 years old is for the children to grow up with an ever-deepening understanding of the natural laws that govern our planet, and of designs for living in harmony with them.* It is one of the attributes of the human being that he can manipulate, change, and even in a small way create, his own living environment as no other organism has ever been able to do, and with the most far-reaching consequences. Therefore, it is as important for the ordinary person to understand the base rules of our existence as it is for him to be able to read, write, and calculate. In the matter of survival, it may prove to be more so.

We do not attempt to teach mathematics without laying down a considerable groundwork of practical, concrete activity and experience, yet we still expect children to understand complex, abstract, scientific ideas without any similar basis of concrete experience to precede it. Chapter 1 illustrates the way in which field studies of a very simple kind with quite young children can be used as a basis for later, more formal, experimental work. Do you remember as a child, doing a series of experiments about photosynthesis and respiration without quite grasping their significance? Did they give you an understanding of a vital relationship that has coloured your conscious thinking ever since? They should have done! These and many other scientific concepts failed to become part of our thinking partly because we did not do the concrete groundwork first, and because we did not grow up with them. Unless we were lucky, we were presented with abstract concepts in isolation, as part of an examination syllabus, when they should have become part of our ABC of living. The vital work for the infant, junior, and middle school is to bring children up with ideas that will become critically examined and fully developed in the upper school so that they become a significant and usable part of the ordinary person's educational equipment. This includes the essentials of historical, philosophical, and geographical, as well as of scientific thinking. The press and other media are much occupied these days with survival, especially since in many parts of the world even survival at a low level has become difficult. Our children will live through a time of tremendous change, and competition for the world's resources will grow more fierce. Because man is inventive, and can manipulate his environment, we may expect more and more elegant solutions to energy problems, and these will be the product of real intellectual achievement. Unfortunately, if present trends persist, we shall see the development of more and more sophisticated means of human destruction as well. There will be demands for change, in the places in which we live, the way we live, and in the work we do (or do not have to do!). Hence the need for the teacher to be able to take children, in simple, direct ways that they will understand, below the surface in their studies. Such an approach involves thinking based upon first-hand field work.

We may be in danger of confusing survival with living. Rules for survival, for individuals and species, are clear, although in communities we may not yet find ourselves able to live within them.

Living is much more than this; and learning to live in harmony with our surroundings and fellow people—to share, to inspire others, and to be inspired—needs a philosophy as well as rules. A teacher's own philosophy (even the lack of one) will come out clearly in his work with the children. No doubt the author's comes out clearly in this book!

Science can provide us with the inescapable rules within which we have to live; geography provides us with the skills to classify, explore, and interpret our environment. Time and history are bound up in our attitudes, and, again, their study in the junior school is developed in practical ways through field study. Each of these studies, the scientific, the geographical, and the historical, has its own way of thinking; all three can be explored and developed with younger children.

There are many philosophies for living. The Book of Genesis tells us that God created man for two purposes; firstly to worship Him and be His friend and companion, and secondly to be His steward, looking after, and enjoying, the fair Earth He created. A small girl, told of this, said thoughtfully, 'Then God didn't make a very good job of man, did He?' This is a questionable statement, but we can see what she meant, for if it is true, man appears to have turned his back on the first function and to have exploited the second for his own ends. One person's religion may permeate the whole of his relationship with his surroundings in every aspect, as it should in the case of a Christian; another person has no obvious religious belief, yet clearly cares for and lives in harmony with his environment. Yet another would seem to be willing to exploit anything to gain his own ends. All this is true of communities, as well as of individuals; and the exploration of man's attitudes and living styles, past and present, local, national, and international should be part of our environmental study from an early age, again, in as practical a way as possible. This means starting with people and things we know. The school environment is full of practical clues to the philosophies of living of past generations (see Chapters 6 and 7).

As far as we know, we differ from all other organisms in being creatively aware of our environment, in appreciating light and shade, shape and form, and growth and movement. These can be interpreted and explored in many different concrete and abstract ways, including drawing, modelling, poetry, drama, and music. In an integrated study, the work should flow naturally from the more academic thinking and information-gathering into the more creative activities.

Valuable first-hand study involves a freedom, freedom to write, to draw, to make diagrams, which only comes naturally in very few children. For most children it has to be learned by working alongside the teacher, who is performing the same skills. This leads to a study in some depth, in which observations are joined together and patterns appreciated. This is where the teacher's role and understanding are so vital, for the patterns can be of many kinds.

A criticism of many of the large and brightly illustrated children's books that have flooded the market today is that they are superficially attractive; they can, and sometimes have to, take the place of first-hand experience, but they are not sufficiently detailed to act as reference books. Throughout this book it is suggested that children should come fairly late in their investigation to books, which can then be used in confirmation and extension of what has already been discovered.

Educational efficiency

Early in this chapter we looked at an equation. Educational efficiency (the best gain for the least input in terms of time, staffing, and resources) is being looked at more closely than ever before. There is no doubt that if our environmental curriculum is to include first-hand study, frequent field visits will be necessary, often involving small numbers of children. These have to be justified and it is suggested that each visit is looked at carefully using an equation like the one shown in Fig. 3.1. On one side we put down *all* the resources that will go into the visit. On the other side we analyse the gain closely and honestly, in terms of, for example, new knowledge and experience, previous knowledge reinforced, skills learned and practised. We then make a judgement as to whether the visit is worthwhile, or whether its purpose could be accomplished in some more efficient way.

Scope of the study

Our study started with a single blackberry in a bramble patch and then passed through a ditch; it goes on to take in walls and hedgerows and looks at the development of a topic from an ancient rock. It then makes an excursion into time-study and history in a churchyard and church, considers the historical evidence in a parish, and passes to a study of the local community. Wherever we look, we find patterns and order, from the movement of molecules in the making of a blackberry to the building of an ancient church. Sometimes they are expressed in poetry, sometimes mathematically, in beautiful lines, in quick impressions, shapes and colours; in others, in time.

A local inventory of resources

As demonstrated in Chapter 1, many schools have, even within their own grounds, resources that are unused, the value of which is not appreciated. The school and its grounds can often be enriched at little cost, even in a large town. Within one kilometre of school, further resources can be listed, and again within a radius of five kilometres, as shown in the example on page 40. Local people, working and retired, can provide valuable, original resource material.

SCHOOL BUILDING AND GROUNDS

Building style, date	Open grass
Building materials	Trees
Walls	Cultivated areas
Playground areas	Neglected areas
Hedges/hedgerows	Wild areas to be left

Possible enrichment with:

Logs, boulders	Greenhouse
Corrugated iron sheets	Pond, etc.
Bird tables/nesting boxes	Cultivated/wild plots

WITHIN 1 KILOMETRE

Roads, street names	Waste land
Footpaths	Dated buildings
Trees/woods	Shops
Hedges	Houses
Walls	Churches
Ponds/streams	Churchyard
Cultivated areas	Memorials

WITHIN 5 KILOMETRES

All the above, plus:

Parks	Museums
Farms	Archaeological sites
Industry	Sources of parish records

Each of these to have cards in an index.

PEOPLE

Parents, tradesmen, retired local people, etc., to visit, receive visitors, tape interviews, provide material, etc.:

Public services	*Farming/industry*
Fire	Shepherd
Police	Farmer
Ambulance	Blacksmith
Nurse	Hurdlemaker
Postman	Potter
Lifeboatman	
Local clergymen	

Amenities, trade
Shopkeepers
Park-keepers
Librarian
Archaeologist

Retired people
Local historians
Retired tradesmen
(e.g., wall-builders)

The idea is to build up, as part of the school's resources, a card index of all likely places and people, and to use those nearest the school for any particular purpose. Once started, the index will be added to steadily, with contributions from staff, children, and parents.

Summary

This book works from the point of view that environmental study provides an essential base for the curriculum of children to the age of 12 or 13; that it is an integrated study in which although subject boundaries are not at all important, the ideas and methodologies of the different disciplines are used as tools of investigation and learning (Fig. 3.2).

It is suggested that the purposes of environmental study embrace the education of children for an understanding of the laws and principles that govern our living and progress. These would include rules for survival, and knowledge from which to make informed judgements, a study of philosophies of living, so that the individual can develop his own in an informed way, from knowledge rather than through ignorance, and a development of aesthetic appreciation of the environ-

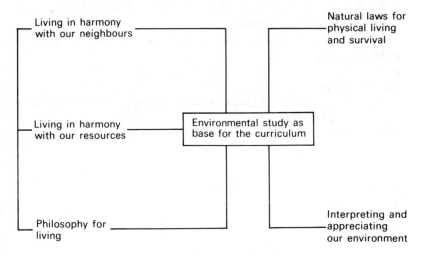

Fig. 3.2   Environmental study as a base for the curriculum

ment, and especially of the individual's gifts and skills in its interpretation. Learning experiences should be selected throughout the earlier school years, to ensure a balance of skills, experience, and knowledge gained, and to ensure that what is done is appropriate at each stage of the child's development.

The school and its immediate locality should be exploited to the full for first-hand teaching and fieldwork, having regard to the time and resources involved, and the subsequent educational gain. It is expected that visits farther afield could be reduced, and that when they are undertaken, their purposes would be clearly locked in with the school's scheme of study, and there would be an extension of experience that could not be gained in any other way.

Bibliography

*Strongly recommended

ENVIRONMENTAL STUDIES

*HARLEN, W. and EMNEVER, L. (1974) *With Objectives in Mind, Schools Council Science 5–13 Project*, Macdonald Educational, London.

HARRIS, M. and EVANS, M. (1971) *Case Studies, Schools Council Environmental Studies Project*, Hart Davis, London.

HARRIS, M., EVANS, M., and REES, G. (1971) *Teachers Guide, Schools Council Environmental Studies Project*, Hart Davis, London.

*PERRY, G. A., JONES, E., and HAMMERSLEY, A. (1972) *Environmental Studies, Teachers Guide Book No. 1, Schools Council Science 5–13 Project*, Blandford, London.

Portesham Environmental Studies Pilot Scheme. See Chapter 5 Bibliography.

BASIC CONCEPTS

British Museum (Natural History) (1978) *Nature at Work*, Cambridge University Press, Cambridge.

*STORER, J. H. (1963) *The Web of Life*, Vincent Stuart, London.

4. Walls and hedges

Walls and hedges usually follow man-made boundaries, although they were frequently built to keep animals in or people out. They can be unsuspected storehouses of local history, geography, and geology, and they can provide both highly specialized and very general places in which wild plants and animals can flourish. A school is lucky indeed if such a wall or hedge forms part of its own boundary, for then part of it can be permanently marked off, and a detailed study of it made over many years.

Walls are entirely man-made, with varying degrees of skill; hedges grow more or less quickly, according to the shrubs used. Both are examples of a vertical habitat, although they are very different in the forms of life they support. In some ways, a wall can be regarded as a cliff in miniature. A hedge is managed from year to year; a wall is left to itself for years.

Urban and suburban hedges, even in parks, often consist of one kind of plant, for example, laurel, privet, or hawthorn. They are (or were, when manpower was cheaper) ruthlessly pruned and kept neat and tidy. As we shall see, these hedges are very different from those found in mature countryside. If some of the hedges in towns can be disappointing, stone walls, even in city centres, are often most rewarding. The variety extends from the decayed ruins beside canals and rivers, the stonework of churchyards and neglected buildings, to the impressive, ancient town walls of a place like York. A card index of walls and hedges, and a large scale reference map ought to feature in the school's stocklist of resources.

A city wall

In the years following the Second World War, Bristol provided among its extensive ruins, a remarkable variety of stone walls. Many of these have disappeared during redevelopment, but even in the centre of the city today, walls are to be found at many little, neglected sites, in which well-matched colonies of wild plants and animals—small, balanced *communities*—live out their lives through the seasons, unseen and unregarded. Many of these organisms can be grown at school under artificial conditions, reproduced from the wild state, and, like the blackberries in Chapter 1, have fascinating stories waiting to be unravelled.

Quite near the centre of Bristol is a fairly high stone wall that used to be within easy reach of at least three schools. The stones were large, mostly carboniferous limestone, almost certainly from one of the Mendip quarries nearby, fairly roughly faced and hewn, and bound together with cement. The colour varied, some of the stones being surfaced with patches of small, coarse crystals that glittered in the sun; others were covered, raised, and indented with strange shapes and markings, some of which made quite passable rubbings. With the aid of a lens these were found to be fragments of fossil shells and crinoid skeletons (Fig. 4.1(a), (b)), plant-like colonial animals whose descendants flourish in present day seas.

Limestone exists in many forms—crystals, marble, chalk, stalactites—which look different from each other and have different properties; yet, chemically, they are all the same substance, namely, calcium carbonate. The time-scale over which they became stone is so vast that, in terms of millions of years, it means almost nothing to us. Similarly, the number of carbon and oxygen atoms locked up in the stone over those millions of years is so vast as to be meaningless, and yet, as with the coal mentioned in Chapter 2, there was a time in the distant past when those same atoms moved in and out of trees, ferns, and a host of animals.

It is some of these animals that are enshrined as fossils. There are detailed casts of the original shapes, but without a trace of the original animal left, except for a fragment of shell, and that is calcium carbonate, too.

The top of the wall was covered with rough cement, pitted with many shallow cavities where the rain-water lingered. Two or three kinds of moss had become established there, together with a tiny, dried-up groundsel, a willow herb with fiery red stems and leaf tips, and a few patches of thin, golden lichen.

The sides of the wall had their cavities, too, from which protruded little dried-up ferns, a waxy plant called pennyroyal ('belly-buttons' to a generation of children brought up to make up appropriate names when they do not know the real ones), and the shiny leaves and purple–white flowers of the ivy-leaved toadflax. All these plants, and the little animals who also inhabit the crevices have the same problem to overcome, that is, the wall regularly dries out completely.

The immediate surroundings—the stone, scraps of soil, moisture, and the air—constitute the plant's *environment*, that is, the sum-total of all

Fig. 4.1 (a), (b) Stone wall showing crinoids and other fossils

the factors that influence the organism. The seed sown on stony ground in the parable dried up and failed to germinate. That is what happens to most of the seeds that drop on walls, but just a few are sufficiently well *adapted to their environment* to survive and even to flourish. Birds, squirrels, and mice ensure a ready supply of seeds on top of the wall; even the wind adds its share. If you doubt this, sweep up the dust from the top of the wall with a clean paint brush. Sow it thinly on a sterilized seed compost, keep it moist and warm, and see what happens. Plants appear able to grow out of the tiniest crevices, even without soil. Lichens (Kershaw and Alvin, 1963) are interesting both because they consist of two kinds of plant (an alga and a fungus) growing intermingled to look like one, and because their presence is an indication of air purity. Lichens do not grow in any quantity in polluted air. Colonies on walls grow slowly; their increase can be measured from year to year by placing permanent peg markers and fitting clear polyglaze over them to draw round the colony each year. As they grow slowly, some wall lichens produce a kind of acid that dissolves the rock; these fragments combine with the slowly rotting lichen tissue to form a poor, thin covering of humus.

In an area of high pollution wall lichens will probably be nonexistent; in a deep rural area, or even a clean air (smokeless) zone, a wall may be heavily encrusted grey, black, and orange, with several different kinds of lichen. The organization WATCH has available a pollution study kit based partly on the presence or absence of lichens.

The stone wall is a *habitat* (Fig. 4.2(a), (b)), always having particular environmental features, e.g., regular drying up, temperature fluctuation, and lack of soil. We should look upon the plant and animal occupants of a particular habitat as a kind of family, whose members live and grow together, and depend on each other. They are a *community*, affected by common outside influences, but supporting each other from within. Children should be encouraged to look at particular habitats as a whole: the living organisms, the inorganic features, and the climatic and soil factors. The examples given, a moss and a snail (Fig. 4.3(a), (b)), are just two of many organisms associated with a stone wall; even small children can be encouraged to see how such organisms can flourish in an inhospitable environment.

Ivy-leaved toadflax is a former garden plant that is particularly adapted to living on walls. Its long, thin flower stalk at first responds to light by bending the flower towards it; later, when the seeds have formed, the stalks point away from the light, moving the capsule inwards, so that when it opens, the seeds stand a good chance of being projected into the wall cavities.

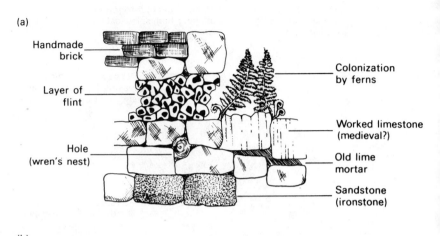

(a)

Handmade brick

Layer of flint

Hole (wren's nest)

Colonization by ferns

Worked limestone (medieval?)

Old lime mortar

Sandstone (ironstone)

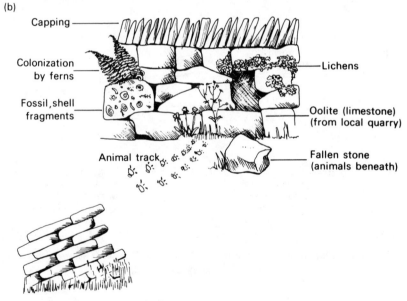

(b)

Capping

Colonization by ferns

Fossil, shell fragments

Lichens

Oolite (limestone) (from local quarry)

Animal track

Fallen stone (animals beneath)

Purbeck wall – stones on incline

Fig. 4.2 (a) Part of a boundary wall in Salisbury. (b) Detail of Cotswold dry stone wall

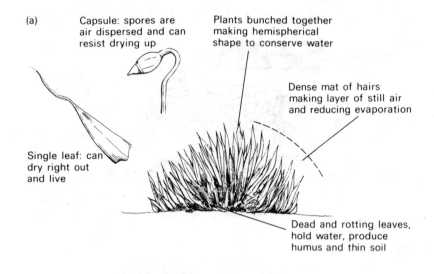

(a) Capsule: spores are air dispersed and can resist drying up

Plants bunched together making hemispherical shape to conserve water

Dense mat of hairs making layer of still air and reducing evaporation

Single leaf: can dry right out and live

Dead and rotting leaves, hold water, produce humus and thin soil

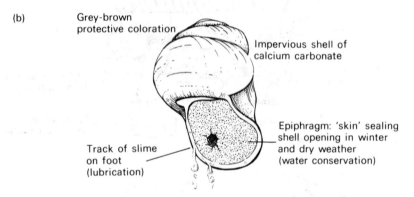

(b) Grey-brown protective coloration

Impervious shell of calcium carbonate

Epiphragm: 'skin' sealing shell opening in winter and dry weather (water conservation)

Track of slime on foot (lubrication)

Fig. 4.3 Adaptation to environment: (a) grey wall moss (Grimmia sp.), (b) small snail, living on walls

In Chapter 1, we looked for relationships in the study of blackberries. If we seek carefully, we can find all the stages in the formation of soil on an old stone wall. Fig. 4.4 shows this development in diagram form.

In microcosm, this is how all soils are originally formed. By building a stone wall in the school grounds, or even a 'sample' in a polythene case (to avoid drying up) in the classroom, all these stages can be observed. Mini-habitats like the tree stump (Chapter 2), the stone wall, and the small pond are very much to be encouraged in school grounds, and even home gardens.

There is a great temptation to take a few loose stones out of a damaged wall, thus weakening it, and damaging it still further. Few things enrage a landowner more than to see his stone walls steadily disappear to schools up and down the country. A wall cannot be (*should never be*) taken to pieces to provide specimens, or stone for buildings. Drawings, annotated diagrams, rubbings, and photographs can all provide a lively record of the wall, without taking it down! Like all geological sites today, stone walls, once their interesting features are recognized, come under considerable pressure, and teachers need to be familiar with the Geology Code, published by the Geological Society. Quite apart from damage to the wall, it should be remembered that an unsafe wall can fall upon a child!

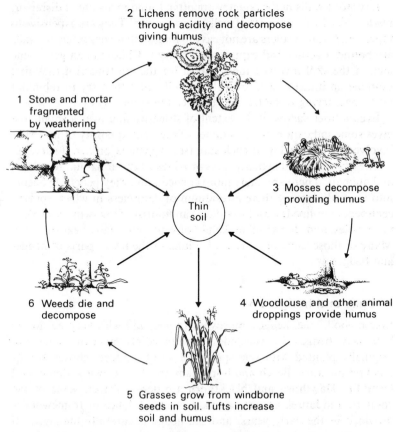

Fig. 4.4 Stages in the development of soil on a stone wall

Spoil heaps are a different matter. Where demolition has taken place, fragments of fossil-bearing and other rock can be easily and safely obtained.

Free-stone walls

In many parts of the country, the walls are not held together with mortar or cement at all. In the Lake District, for example, houses and barns are commonly built of *dry stone* walling. Where stone is plentiful the field boundaries are constructed of dry stone walling, which can often be seen vanishing into the distance right over the steep top of fell or mountain. The pattern and design of construction is characteristic of each area, walls being built quite differently in Purbeck, the Cotswolds (see Fig. 4.2(b)), and the Peak District, for example.

Dry stone walls in the country are often found in a state of disrepair, made worse by the ravages of walkers and others. They are expensive to repair, and stone-wallers are not easy to find, so that very often the walls are bound together and capped with cement. Children can gain some idea of the skill involved (and respect for the craftsman) if they first examine an intact stretch of wall carefully, and then try to rebuild a fallen one, trying to match and balance the stones by eye.

Even a brief survey of the extent of stone-walling over a small area gives some indication of the number of men and quantity of materials involved in the heyday of enclosure (see Appendix on aerial survey).

The dry stone wall in many ways provides an easier habitat for plants and animals. There are many more crevices, and they penetrate deeply into the wall, leaving there a residuum of dampness in which spiders, centipedes, millipedes, and woodlice can flourish. Slow-worms, snakes, mice, voles, and shrews all make use of walls, especially near the base. Many of those same organisms also inhabit the lower parts of hedges and hedgerows.

Hedges and hedgerows

Like a good wine, hedges improve with age, and with keeping. Many boundary hedges by roadsides are incredibly ancient. They are originally planted with one species of shrub or tree, chosen for its quickset qualities. Beech and hornbeam are slow growing, dense, and beautiful. Hawthorn and blackthorn are dense. Privet, some of the conifers, and laurel, are very quick growing. A fence or framework is provided in the early years, and the hedge is carefully managed. In former times the hedges (miles of them!) were regularly thinned and layered, leaving them dense at the base with large trunks. Because labour is so expensive, layering is not a common sight these days. Jennings (1978) has a good, simple account of layering, with drawings.

As the hedge increases in age, the bank and ditch usually associated with it become riddled with holes and covered in rubbish and detritus of various kinds. Other species of trees and shrubs grow up, some of them being allowed to grow tall, providing windbreaks and shelter for many kinds of animals.

Rabbits, voles, moles, even foxes and badgers, make an old hedgerow into a veritable warren of holes and passages. Soil thrown out, stones, and bones of former occupants have served to build up the base of the hedgerow, providing not only shelter for the legitimate occupants, but also homes for many kinds of snail, spider, beetle, and woodlouse. The turned over soil provides, with the shelter of the hedge, just the right conditions for a whole variety of hedgerow flowers, that are not so obviously, nor as closely, adapted to their environment as those that survive on stone walls. The very names, for example, hedge bedstraw, hedge parsley, Jack-by-the-hedge, hedge woundwort, tell of the long association between flowers and hedgerows; in three of these, the name even suggests their former use.

Hedgerow studies

These can be divided between an intensive seasonal study over several years (with different groups of children) of a short stretch of hedge, say 20 metres (Fig. 4.5), and a more general study of the use, history, and management of hedges over a wider area, remembering that we are looking all the time for patterns and relationships.

SINGLE STRETCH OF HEDGE

The simplest way to study the hedge is to keep a diary through the year, consisting of observations, drawings, photographs, and short pieces of writing. This has some literary value, and a pleasant volume can be produced in this way, but there is a considerable danger of superficiality, unless the observations made are further developed to some purpose. Temperatures can be taken daily at various fixed points, and a study (varying with the age of the children), made of the microclimate and its effect on life in the hedge. (See Chapter 3 for more details.) Charts can be made and compared annually of the dates of emergence of leaves, flowers, and fruits of common species. Small, documented collections are mentioned in Chapter 3. A mature hedge and hedgerow may provide up to fifty flowering plants, samples of which can be very simply

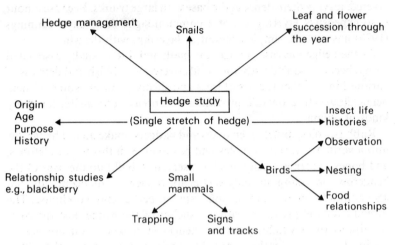

Fig. 4.5   Hedge and hedgerow studies

mounted on standard cards, using a transparent adhesive plastic, like that used for covering books. Provided the plants are dry, the process is instant, requiring no pressing.

An apology is necessary for coming back to snails. The hedgerow and hedge on a damp night are full of them. They can be studied alive, and their shells can be collected when they have died.

Much work has been done on the marking and studying of individual animals, and most of it, like the singing of birds, and the tagging of small mammals is unsuitable for younger children. However, it is very easy to mark snails with a quick-drying enamel paint, using a fine brush, and either a colour code or numbers, and thus follow the movements of the individuals, and sometimes their fate! There are many more different kinds of land snail than one might suppose (Kerney and Cameron, 1979), some of them with unsuspected shapes. Snail shells, even when damaged, are not easily destroyed; sharp-eyed children will find many empty shells and with the aid of one or two recent good books (McMillan, 1973), they can be identified, giving a clue to the range of living snails present. Again, a small, instant collection of shells can be built up, annotated in detail, and added to.

Trapping

There are many possibilities in hedges for trapping animals of all kinds. Some forms of trapping (e.g., of birds) are best left to experts, and it is important to realize that when we trap any animal, we assume responsibility for its welfare.

For example, small mammals (mice, voles, shrews) can be trapped either with the commercial Longworth, live trap, or by one of several home-made variations of it. The trapped animal may die if it has to undergo extremes of heat or cold, lack of food or water, so the traps need to be visited frequently, and all precautions taken when they are set. In this way, an enthusiastic teacher can obtain common and bank voles, field mice, and common shrews, to be kept for a very short time in an aquarium for observation and drawing before being released again. Individuals (especially voles) rapidly become used to traps, and are often caught again and again. Size of eyes and whiskers, length of tail, condition of coat, protective coloration should all be noted. Any teacher who undertakes trapping of vertebrates is urged to attend a course before doing so.

It is important to note that *it is illegal to keep in captivity most wild birds and mammals, and even when kept for an hour or two for study, they should not be handled by the children, since infection is possible.*

Various kinds of pot trap can be set, usually in the form of glass jars let into the ground so that the lip lies just below the ground level. Animals, particularly nocturnal ones, then fall into the jar, but are prevented by the smooth sides and the shoulder from getting out. Again, the traps need to be attended to frequently, to prevent suffering. Beetles, harvestmen, and many other invertebrates can be caught in this way.

One kind of, often fatal, pot trap will be found in many roadside hedges. Picnickers and holidaymakers throw away large numbers of glass jars and bottles, especially milk bottles, that frequently fall at an angle which enables animals to enter but not to leave. Many of these bottles contain the remains of small mammals and invertebrates that have died there.

Language work is often concentrated on birds and flowers, and possibly trees, whereas small invertebrates, especially when watched for a while with a lens or a low-power binocular microscope, can stimulate a wide vocabulary and considerable powers of description. The smaller we go in scale, the more surprises await us. A very careful study of leaf litter will often produce a false scorpion, a creature up to 3 mm long which resembles its big cousin almost exactly except that it has no tail. There are numerous kinds of false scorpion; one man spent much of his life writing a book about them!

Naming plants and animals

In Chapter 3, we discussed briefly the identification of plants and animals. Many of them have ancient common names, for example, dormouse and badger. Most large plants and animals have genuinely common names by which they have been known for generations. Some groups, like the grasses, have well-established names because of their connection with farming. Yorkshire fog, meadow fescue, cocksfoot, and the foxtails are just a few of the well-known grasses. Slugs and snails have more exotic names, for example how did the pellucid glass snail and the two-toothed door snail get their names?

Names can be misleading. Similar names can refer to animals from totally different families. White bryony and black bryony both have greenish flowers, are climbers, and are found in hedges; but the former belongs to the cucumber family and the latter is the sole British representative of the yams!

Earlier in this chapter we noted an invented name ('belly-buttons' for the wall-plant pennyroyal). There is nothing wrong with invented names, since every name had to be invented at some time, and we may encourage children to invent appropriate ones but it must be remembered that they only have local value.

It was the great Swedish naturalist Linnaeus who invented a system for naming which could be unique and international.

He placed all the plants and animals he could examine into families, usually according to their external similarities. These he divided into smaller groups called *genera*. The members of each genus carried the same forename. Thus, the members of the Maple *genus* are all called *Acer . . .*; common maple is *Acer campestre* while sycamore is *Acer pseudoplatanus*. The second is the *specific* name, and the plant is a *species*. These names were given by Linnaeus in the eighteenth century and are still in use today. Linnaeus used Latin and Greek because they were understood internationally. Like all great inventions, this naming system was only an extension of something very simple. You might say my generic name is Prosser, my specific name is Peter, and my subspecific name is John.

This international system of naming enables people all over the world to refer to the same plant. This brings us back to how the pellucid glass snail and the two-toothed door snail got their names: they are direct translations from the Latin!

Hedges and history

Pollard, Hooper, and Moore (1968) provide a fine background book for the teacher. Chapters 2 and 3 of their book give an account of the origins of hedges and their early history, with which it is possible to compare the hedge pattern of one's own area. In Chapter 5 it is pointed out that hedges have recently been removed on an alarming scale. This is where a simple aerial survey, even a single photograph, taken under good conditions, can reveal not only the present pattern of hedges in the study area, but the routes of the hedges which have been taken out. Slight variations in soil, humidity, and vegetation mark them out even years later. (See Appendix on aerial survey at end of this chapter.) The aerial photograph can be compared with patterns shown by old maps. We found an 1844 tithe map in the Church records that showed all our local fields, although their use had been considerably changed over the years. It is not easy for younger children to go beyond a simple comparison between the photographs, the map, and what they see on the ground.

Dr Hooper, working on the principle that a hedge is usually planted with one species, and that the older it is, the more kinds of trees and shrubs will have become established in it, and by doing a lot of detailed comparison with hedges whose dates could be fixed from other sources, suggested a simple mathematical formula that could be applied to a 30-metre sample of hedge (averaged from several, under careful conditions). This would give a rough idea of the age of the hedge, distinguishing, for example, between modern, eighteenth century, Tudor, and Saxon hedges.

When our twelve-year-olds applied this to the hedge that follows the road to the north of our school boundary, they estimated it to be around 600 years old. It could well have originated as the boundary along an ancient trackway in the early fourteenth century, when large scale sheep enclosures took place. As we shall see in Chapter 6, a number of other important structures in the area seem to come from about the same date.

It is easy to move from the realm of historical evidence to that of speculation. We would have to test the age given by Hooper's formula against the actual evidence, if any, of parish and other records, and the likelihood of that age set against what is known generally of the period. From quite an early age, children can develop a critical faculty in coming to conclusions from data of all kinds, but devised by themselves, at first hand.

Management of hedges

'Hedging and ditching' used to be a traditional farm skill, but it is rarely seen in its original form today. Every few years the hedge was thinned and layered, with the retained saplings staked horizontally to vertical poles; new growth was then able to thicken outwards, to be trimmed in the intervening years. The outlines of a possible school hedge survey are given in an appendix to Pollard, Hooper, and Moore (1968). When the information has been obtained, it is possible, according to the ages of the children, to look at the present day value of hedges, in particular the conflict between the farmer's need to gain his livelihood from the land in the most economical way, and the management of the hedges for their amenity value, that is for their aesthetic qualities and as a major reservoir for wild life.

What methods are used for cutting hedges in the area under survey? Does the hedge untidily cut back with a modern flail regenerate quickly? What proportion of local hedges are being allowed to grow up unmanaged? What is the actual *function* of the remaining hedges, as we see it? Is the hedgerow vegetation controlled by chemicals? How often is it cut back? Could the need for economy, and therefore less frequent cutting, be a good thing?

It is good to come back from such broad considerations to the small stretch of hedge we study intensively, and look at numbers of organisms in the hedge. How much can it be called a reservoir for wild life? Exactly *what* kinds of bird use it? Do they gain their food from it, and if so, what do they feed on? This is where we carry on from the simple identification, and the superficial study, into a look at causes and effects. The lessons we learned in Chapter 1 about energy-exchange and food cycles can be applied in a simple way to the relationships of a hedge, and sooner or later we have to see if a case can be made for the retention of a hedge which is stronger than the farmer's case for wanting to remove it. It is at this point that a farmer may be asked to come into school and discuss their findings with the children. If the discussion is taped—and hopefully it might lead to a visit to the farm for the specific purpose of looking at the hedges—a display can be made putting the two sides of the argument, for and against removing hedges.

In studying their local environment, it is important for the children to come directly, and at first hand, against the conflicting factors regarding usage and change. In a town this is often highlighted by 'developments', especially where they concern a change in use of previously open land. In more rural areas, the hedges and hedgerows provide an easily studied point of clear conflict, and it is part of our children's education for them to learn to compile their own information and, in the light of it, look at arguments for and against what is proposed.

Summary

Stone walls are an example of a highly specialized *habitat* that provides an *environment* in which only certain kinds of plant and animal are *adapted* to live. Hedges and hedgerows, living and changing, provide a much less specialized habitat in which a whole variety of plants and animals live together.

Walls are good for study, partly because they contain so few organisms. Dry stone walls vary according to the part of the country; boundaries are usually predominantly walls, or hedges, but rarely mixed. Both can be surveyed with the aid of local maps.

Named hedges and hedgerows are compact nature reserves for study. Collecting, naming, marking, and mapping can all be practised on a small scale.

Collecting data and applying a formula to the dating of hedges is a good introduction to a critical study of the accuracy and limitations of survey methods, and of drawing conclusions. Hedges may be a fixed sequence point (see Chapter 6). They may be one of several gateways to the study of local history.

APPENDIX: The Aerial Survey

It is well worth getting acquainted with a member of a local flying club, since an hour's flying in a light, high-winged aircraft can produce a survey of the whole area round the school. An ordinary 35 mm camera loaded with fairly fast film can be used, the best time being early morning or late afternoon on a day when the air is clear, with very little mist about. Using an ordinary 5 cm lens and a shutter speed of 1/250 s, and height of 300–450 m, the area is covered by flying along a pre-arranged grid. The perspex window of the aircraft needs to be clean, and the camera lens should be as near it as possible without actually touching it. (If it does touch, vibration occurs.)

Not only do hedges and walls cast a shadow but often it is possible to pick out clearly the route of former hedges even when they have been taken out years before. The photographs are interpreted beside a large-scale ordnance survey map, and a wall and hedge map can be constructed (Fig. 4.6).

Aerial photograph of fields near school from approx 450 m

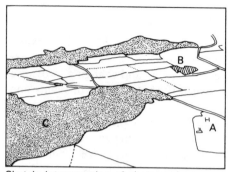

Sketch: interpretation of photograph

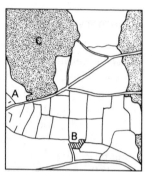

Sketch map (1:25,000)
based on ordnance survey
of area photographed

Points of reference:
A   Corner of school field
B   Holwell Farm
C   Burwood

.... Indicates where hedges
have been removed

Fig. 4.6   Aerial photograph and interpretation: part of a field and hedgerow
survey

References

HIRONS, J. and C. (eds.) (1980) 'Up the wall', *Wildlife Education*, summer, 1980.

JENNINGS, T. (1978) *The Story of a Hedge*, Faber and Faber, London.

KERNEY, M. P., CAMERON, R. A. D., and RILEY, G. (1979) *A Field Guide to the Land Snails of Britain and N.W. Europe*, Collins, London.

KERSHAW, K. A. and ALVIN, K. L. (1963) *The Observers Book of Lichens*, Warne, London.

MCMILLAN, N. F. (1973) *British Shells*, Warne, London.

POLLARD, E., HOOPER, M. D., and MOORE (1968) *Hedges, Collins New Naturalist Series*, Collins, London.

PRIME, C. T. (1963) *The Young Botanist*, Nelson, London. (See Chapter 8, Walls and hedgerows.)

SOUTHWOOD, T. R. E. (1963) *Life of the Wayside and Woodland*, Warne, London.

Bibliography

Council for Environmental Education, *Hedges* (bibliography). See Addresses.

Council for Environmental Education, *The Wall* (booklet). See Addresses.

LEIGH-PEMBERTON, J. (1980) *Hedges*, Ladybird Books, Loughborough, Leicestershire.

Addresses

Council for Environmental Education, School of Environmental Education, Reading University, London Road, Reading, RG21 5AQ.

Geologists Association, c/o Geology Department, University College London, Gower Street, London, WC1E 6BJ.

WATCH, 22 The Green, Nettleham, Lincoln, LN2 2NR.

5. Flint: an integrated study

An oak tree had been growing in the village school playground for longer than anyone could remember. The gale that brought it crashing down one autumn night, took out with it a stretch of the playground wall that dated, like the school, from mid-Victorian times. Next morning found us, from the school up the road, searching for treasure in the rubble.

There was flint in abundance, together with handmade, local brick and tiling, ironstone, sandstone, and fragments of previously used limestone, all held together with clumps of lichen-covered lime mortar.

In our part of the country, chalk and flint are more common than anything else. The rounded hills, the lack of surface water, the particular trees and shrubs that grow, the very changing colours of the fields, are all influenced by massive chalk deposits, laid down in a pure form over millions of years in the clear, tranquil seas that covered the very spot where we live and work. Nobody has yet succeeded fully in explaining how the flint got among the chalk, but if the chalk influences the landscape, flint certainly influences the traditional walls and buildings, though it is not an easy material to build with.

Bed-rock and subsoil

Every place, whether it is in the town or the country, is built over bed-rock and subsoil, all of which are visible in places, and influence the landscape to a greater or lesser degree. Whilst the influences of soil and subsoil are usually more clearly seen in the countryside than in the town (the red soil of Devon fields and motorway cuttings, the dour granite of Dartmoor, and the millstone grit and ancient limestone of Derbyshire come to mind), there are cities like Bristol and Edinburgh where the rock outcrops spectacularly within the city boundary. Bed-rock and soil influence not only the landscape, but the plant and animal development and human usage. The bed-rock is often used as a local building material, as, for example, in Bath and the Pennine towns; in other areas such as the Home Counties it can give rise to man-made building materials, such as brick and tiles. Over a hundred years ago Purbeck and Portland stone were being transported on a large scale to London. With modern transport the direct link between bed-rock and building style has now largely disappeared and a whole new range of modern, often synthetic, building materials has appeared universally. Nevertheless, if we seek out the older parts even of many of our big cities where they have not been completely redeveloped, we may find, still, considerable evidence of the use of local materials in building.

Our bed-rock is chalk, which can be used for many purposes, but is much too soft for building anything but defensive ramparts, for which purpose it was used most successfully in the Bronze and Iron Ages in the construction of a series of elaborate forts that survive to this day. Chalk is too soft, even for building stone walls, so, characteristically, our fields are bounded by hedges, some of them very ancient, as we saw in Chapter 4. The hills have softly rounded contours, the soil is light, well-drained, and alkaline, ideal in fact, for barley. So we could say the chalk has been responsible, in a way, for the removal of miles of hedges to create the very large fields in which modern machinery can be used economically. T. H. Huxley (1868), in a remarkable essay that should be read by any aspiring integrated studies enthusiast, called 'On a piece of chalk', described the chalk country as having 'a peacefully domestic and mutton-suggesting prettiness, which can hardly be called either grand or beautiful . . .'

When we begin to connect cause and effect in this way, we are thinking as a geographer does. We can go on to connect, in our area, the supply of water from deep artesian bores, and the considerable watercress industry made possible by the pollution-free, alkaline water that flows away down our little river to the not too distant sea.

Planning the topic

Like the chalk, and originally embedded in it, flint is abundant in our area. Nodules of it can be picked up in large numbers in the fields without damaging the environment. Because flint and chalk have been built into the very history of our countryside, and its inhabitants, we had been thinking for some time of making it the subject of a large-scale topic study. The principles discussed here, and the ideas developed, could just as well be applied to any other material that has a wide local application. For example, we have worked in a similar way with the nearby clay deposits that gave rise to a distinctive brick and pottery industry over some six hundred years and to a number of local place-names.

The planned topic is very different in scope, execution, and time scale, from the kind of open-ended investigations pursued in Chapters 1 and 2.

Work of that kind may be followed up seasonally, material and records can be built up over years, and the investigation taken up and put aside several times in the year. The larger scale topic is planned ahead to cover a fixed time, and, possibly, to capitalize on high but short-term enthusiasm. A major topic may take years to 'incubate' before everything comes together and the time seems right to develop it.

The teacher's preliminary study may well be based on a single book (as was the study of hedges in Chapter 4), which may give basic knowledge, indicate the scope and possibilities of the study, and reveal the pitfalls.

The book used in this way for the flint topic (Shepherd, 1972) is unfortunately now out of print, but obtainable from libraries. It is a book for teacher rather than children; parts of it are hard-going even for adults. Many children's books deal usually with only one aspect, and then in insufficient detail.

The degree of planning of the topic will vary with the individual, and with the mode of working. The guidelines are laid down, and there are various ways in which the skills can be recorded, for groups and for individual children. The pattern of skills required and practised, and the activities engaged in, will differ from child to child. The topics chosen over a period should reflect a balance of the mathematical, language, scientific, geographical, historical, and philosophical skills and experiences appropriate to each year group. Coordination of the topic cycle through the school ensures that any duplication and overlapping are deliberate, and not accidental. The detailed planning of the topic has not been greatly developed here, since a number of books, notably those of the Science 5–13 series (see Chapter 4 Bibliography), deal with this matter at length.

Flint

When at first we pick up a nodule of flint and break it open, there is nothing to be seen that would turn our thoughts to its very ancient and gradual formation; our imagination does not naturally range over the thirty million or so years during which life forms were constantly dying, deposits being precipitated in a steady shower from their skeletons onto the tranquil sea bed. What we *see* in our hand is a hard, glassy rock, whose surfaces have splintered in a series of graceful curves and sharp edges. We need a good but not too technical book to take us beyond the object in the hand and open our eyes to all its possibilities. Flint should decorate the mantelpiece at home as well as the desk at school, and all sorts of ideas will occur (and need to be noted) once the imagination gets to work.

Shepherd's book reveals straight away a problem concerning the nature and origin of flint. One can describe flint in terms of what it looks and feels like, and its properties, and we learn that it is composed almost entirely of silica, which exists in several other forms, the commonest being in grains of sand. One hundred pages of the book are taken up with the exact nature of flint, and the way in which it *may* have been formed, but we still do not know how all that silica came together to form the hard nodules scattered through the chalk that we know as flint. Silica is not a very soluble substance; a lot of water would contain only a little dissolved silica, yet huge quantities of it seem to have come together in those chalky seas in odd-shaped masses, some of them enveloping fossil shells. Sponges are full of needle-like spicules made of silica which, presumably, they can extract from sea water. Sponges lived in those seas, and there may be a connection between flint and those early sponges. Diatoms and other sea organisms have also been suggested.

It is much easier to say what flint is like, and what is does, than to say precisely what it *is*. Many of our definitions are of this kind. It is good for children to learn that the origin of even so common a substance as flint is still shrouded in mystery.

Properties of flint

Flint is fascinating stuff to handle. The outer layer of the oddly shaped *nodule*, the *cortex*, is hard and powdery, looking just like chalk, but the *core*, with its glassy, smooth surfaces comes in a variety of colours. Can we distinguish the white flint of the cortex from chalk? If powdered and placed under a microscope would they look the same? Are there any simple chemical tests we can apply?

How hard is the flint? How do you measure hardness? We discover that many 'rule of thumb' scales are still very useful. They are comparative, rather than exact. Moh's hardness scale, outlined below, is one of these.

Scale

1. Talc	}	Can be scratched by a finger nail
2. Gypsum		
3. Calcite		Marked by copper coin
4. Fluorspar		Marked by penknife
5. Apatite		Marked by glass
6. Feldspar		Marked by steel file
7. Quartz		Will itself scratch glass
8. Topaz		
9. Corundum		
10. Diamond		

Each mineral will scratch those below it in the scale, and be scratched by those above it. Thus a substance which cannot mark quartz, but is scratched by it is at hardness 7. Where does flint stand on the hardness scale? Here we may pause to think how our more exact scales of measurement came about. The Beaufort wind scale is a comparative one. The Celsius temperature scale is an absolute measure.

We have seen in previous chapters that the material studied is usually less important than the educational ideas and general lessons it brings out. There is a good example of this here, for an essentially practical study of flint leads us into a more general consideration of how we measure and compare properties.

Investigations that involve the use of chemicals and tools should be done with care and precautions. Dilute acid (even vinegar) can be used to distinguish between chalk and the white flint cortex; the bottle should be kept stoppered, and acid added to the test material in a tube standing in a rack. Practical investigations will soon involve chipping and striking the flint; simple goggles should be worn at all times! Good habits, such as orderliness and tidiness of investigation, and of safety, should begin in the junior classroom.

The collection of a large range of examples shows many variations in colour and texture, some having the most delicate fossils embedded in them, others being coloured all shades, from yellow to reddish brown with deposits of sulphur and iron. Fractured flints reveal series of concavities, thin flakes are a beautiful, translucent fawn, and old, exposed cores have gone milky white, flecked with grey. These are all beautiful subjects for drawing and painting (see Fig. 5.1), but surprisingly difficult when you actually attempt it!

To return to our classroom investigations, and in particular the white stuff coating the nodule, we know that dilute acid would cause it to fizz if it were chalk. There would be quite a violent reaction and gas bubbles would be given off; in fact, the gas carbon dioxide, without which green plants are unable to make food (see Chapter 2). No such thing happens with the white coating of flint, so it cannot be chalk. In fact, it is mainly silica, and silica is *silicon dioxide*. Silicon is another of those building units, very similar to carbon in some of its properties, except that the silicon atom joins with two atoms of oxygen to form a hard, almost insoluble solid, while carbon atoms are similarly each joined to two atoms of oxygen to form a rather heavy gas at ordinary temperatures.

Just as flint influenced the whole civilization of man, in the evolution of tools and weapons, so the substance of which it is made is about to influence our own and succeeding generations in ways as yet undreamed of, and that will dwarf everything that flint did for us in its whole history.

Fig. 5.1 A child's drawing of flint

The silicon chip is with us, an infinitely flexible tool of storage and communication, and we are only just beginning to see what far-reaching changes it will bring in our lives.

Integrated study

Did you think when you joined us in picking up those pieces of cool, grey flint from the ruins of the wall that we should range in such a short time from vast primeval seas to a connection with the very latest of modern technology? Imaginative thinking is the basis of any truly *integrated* study, as compared with a *combined* study in which several subject disciplines are brought to bear on a topic from the outside. The combined study looks at a topic in what methods and materials it will provide from the point of view of each of its disciplines. An *integrated* study arises by an imaginative development *from* the topic in hand, using the most appropriate tools and methods that come to light as the investigation proceeds. The same person or group may find themselves thinking at one time as a scientist, at another as a geographer or

65

historian, and at another as a philosopher, choosing and using the most appropriate thinking and practical techniques for the needs of the moment. No one person can be a specialist in everything, and this is why it is so valuable to have experts available for consultation, rather than for direction. There is no great mystery about the different ways of identifying and using the most appropriate tools. A person who does this becomes a craftsman in *learning*. (It is useful to note here that Chapter 1 gives the essentials of scientific thinking, Chapter 6 of historical thinking, and Chapter 8 of geographical thinking, in so far as these can be separated from each other.)

Fig. 5.2 Starting to make flint tools (note the precautions)

From the foregoing, it is obvious that our study of flint could be very wide-ranging, but lacking in depth (as many developed topics are), or it could be narrow in concept, but too deep in its thinking for the age and development of the children. To get it just right, and completed within the time available, requires knowledge of the children, and reflection and planning of the topic material.

Although we start from the concrete, that is, with the collection of nodules of flint from the fields and material from broken walls and a ruined church, it is all too easy to revert very quickly to books. Such second-hand knowledge, copied drawings and writing is best left to a fairly late stage in the topic so that activities, thoughts, and ideas are arrived at and carried out at first hand, especially the writing. During the teacher's research for the topic, visits will be arranged (see Fig. 5.4(a)), and outside helpers sought. Our early thoughts were jotted down as shown in Fig. 5.3 and a concrete study of the properties of flint in the classroom started the topic off (Fig. 5.4(b)).

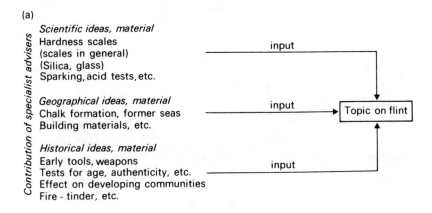

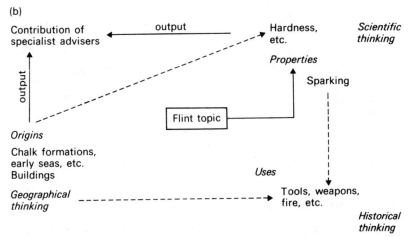

Fig. 5.3 (a) Combined and (b) integrated study of flint

Much of this practical work drew on the kind of scientific thinking developed among the blackberries in Chapter 1, so that we could arrive at a series of statements about flint derived entirely from our own observations. The various properties of flint gave rise to their use by people of many different ages (Fig. 5.5).

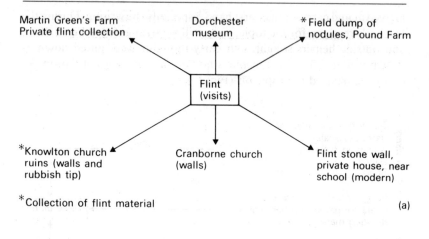

*Collection of flint material

(a)

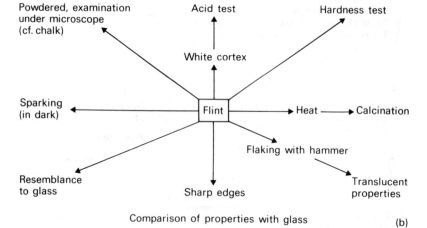

Comparison of properties with glass

(b)

Fig. 5.4 (a) Flint: plan for visits. (b) Flint: a practical investigation

Flint in toolmaking

We are now ready to explore at first hand some of the uses of flint. Tools were an obvious and attractive case in point. A local farmer has a large collection of authentic flints, found in the fields, in the form of axe and arrow heads, and all kinds of domestic implements. Some of these have been restored with wooden shafts and handles. The children can hold the tools, and feel the balance of a finely made tool in the hand. They can go beyond this! With goggles and first-aid box ready, they can try to make tools for themselves, and realize what skill is involved. In doing this, and then in looking at the beautiful leaf finish and symmetry of some of the Neolithic spear heads and axes, they may come to a truer appreciation of the kind of people their ancestors were than is sometimes gained from books.

Our farmer friend not only collects tools, he makes them, using actual toolmaker's cores, perhaps three thousand years old, and the children can watch and listen to his deft movements. The noises of the flint knapper in the hills can also be recorded—a clear, ancient, and resonant sound that must have echoed through the quiet hills for many hundreds of years.

An interesting problem is posed. Some of our friend's tools made fresh from new nodules in the field are so perfect that someone asks why they could not be passed off as the real thing. Would a museum accept a fake as genuine? We attempted this with some pottery once, trying to pass off some of our home-made Iron Age pot shards as genuine, but they deceived no one at the museum.

A freshly split flint is often shiny black in colour, but exposure to the air gradually makes the cut surfaces go white. A really authentic Mesolithic or Neolithic tool, perhaps 4000 years old, will usually have become very light in colour. An expert looks for many other signs, including such delicate refinements as the patina made on flint sickle

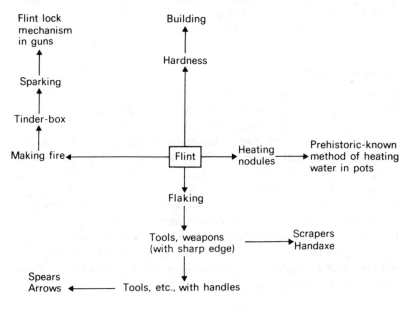

Fig. 5.5 Uses of flint

blades by cutting against so many corn-stems that are heavily impregnated with silica—the same substance as flint—and therefore capable of wearing it away. We have an opportunity here to look in a more general way at what the archaeologist considers to be evidence. With older children, an exploration of the literature of the Piltdown Forgery is salutory (see *Children's Brittanica* (Sales, 1980), under 'Fraud' and *Encyclopaedia Brittanica*).

History

There is an imaginative thrill in just holding a well-balanced flint handtool. One can speculate about the hands that fashioned it, and those that used it. Some children have a very strong sense of historical association. The feel of objects and places, that is, the connection between the present-day hand grasping a handaxe, and that of the original owner. This kind of historical *feel* is immediate in some children but nonexistent in others. It can be shown that few children have any real sense of historical, still less, of geological time but they *can* be given a sense of historical 'feel' by visiting places and handling artefacts. The whole business of the worldwide use of, and trade in, flint tools and weapons is well dealt with in several books and can be followed up as desired, according to the ages and aptitudes of the children, and the time available. The point is that the study *started* with concrete experience of real implements and the children's attempts to make them.

Time sequence

We shall look more closely at the children's idea of time when we look at the churchyard in Chapter 6. Our study of flint introduces both geological and archaeological time scales, as well as historical time. Scaled time-charts can give a *comparative* idea of the time-scales involved, but no real concept of the actual times involved, except to a perceptive few. In a child's mind, there is no difference between ten thousand and ten or a hundred million years, but we are probably wise to start comparisons, *and sequences*, fairly early. It is important to remember that just as a child's sense of time develops gradually over a long period, and to differing degree, so does its sense of scale (see more fully Chapter 6), so that friezes and time-ladders round the room are, with young children, only loosely comparative. This should not inhibit their early introduction into the classroom.

Flint in buildings

When we begin to consider flint as a building material, we move very much into historical time. The parish church and many other older buildings are patterned externally in flint, and a neighbouring church, one whose village has now completely disappeared except in name, is a roofless ruin, the construction of which goes back partly to Norman times. The rubble and flint construction can be seen in the whole width of the broken walls.

The actual flints have hardly become weathered over the years, but we see, in looking at the flint, and in the wall construction (Fig. 5.6), the major problem of flint as a building stone. It is so hard and smooth that mortar only binds to it with difficulty. Hence, flint is used in conjunction with brick and sandstone, which are absorbent, so that the patterns we see are utilitarian, as well as decorative. Modern walls are bound together with cement; all the older walls are bound with lime mortar (with chalk taken from the local chalk pits). Many of the flints were originally fractured, and placed in the wall with the shining black core facing outwards. We found a pile of flints from the ruined medieval wall in which some of the flints had been worked into a 'tang' so as to gain a purchase or hold in the mortar. Again, we tried to convey to the children something of the 'feel' in holding a flint-piece fashioned and shaped by a craftsman some 600 years ago.

We were able to draw a lot of the flint walls *in situ*; some were discoloured, some carried the images of fossils, but we seemed unable to gain any detailed information about the construction of stone walls. That is, until someone thought of Mr Renyard, an elderly gentleman who lives in the village. He, it turned out, had been a stonemason and stone-wall maker all his life; he had actually built a flint stone wall near the school and could show it to us. Invited to school to talk to the children, Mr Renyard turned out to be a natural raconteur. One morning, we taped fifty minutes of his reminiscences, covering the construction and history of flint walls. We learned how, before the turn of the century, farm-workers were 'put off' for the winter, when there was no work for them, and that they then took riddles and baskets into the fields to collect flints for building. They must have worked very hard for little reward. We caught the emotion in our speaker's voice as he compared the application and weathering of traditional lime-mortar which was soon covered in lichens and mosses, with the modern cement used in some local restoration. 'The whole reason they had mortar', he explained, 'was so that it would get covered by lichens and ferns and so on' (see Fig. 5.7). This seemed to him to be important, but the highlight

Fig. 5.6 Ruined flint stone wall

came unexpectedly, when we heard how, as a lad, he had taken a pickaxe to the flagstones in the chancel of our church. We were able to share the moment with him. 'Just think', he said, 'People had worshipped on those stones, and knelt on them for a thousand years—monks and nuns—you could see how they were worn away—and I dug them up!' Here was a man to whom stones were real; they were things to be treated with respect and loving care. And here was a man with a strong sense of historical association.

Fig. 5.7 Close-up of flint stone wall showing mortar and lichens

That tape is a valuable item in our archives. We have the original shut away, and use an edited copy in the classroom. There is still a tremendous quantity of social history and local knowledge to be gained by taped interview with old people, many of whom are best visited by a few children in their own homes. There is an urgency about this: we were always going to interview a former Vice-Chairman of Governors, who was reputed to know more about the history of the area than anyone else (he had been a doctor there for nearly fifty years). Unfortunately, he died, quite suddenly, before we got round to it.

Every local topic ought to provide some permanent material for the school's resource bank. This one yielded a collection of flints of many kinds, a set of slides of implements held in the children's hands, and Mr

Renyard's tape, as well as an interview with the owner of the private museum, and tape of the sounds of flint knapping.

Flint and fire

Flint was, of course, used for hundreds of years to create fire. With suitable precautions, interesting investigations can be done on sparking. Striking steel with a flint, especially if the whole force of the descending flint lands at a tiny point on the steel, makes a fragment of the metal temporarily white hot, causing a spark to fly up. We can experiment with the best way to do this, and with the best material to make tinder (in a tinder-box). Is it possible to devise a method of producing a continuous stream of sparks directed at the tinder? How did old tinder-boxes work? A visit to a local museum produced both tinder-boxes and flint-lock gun mechanisms. These were in use until very recently, and there is a small demand for gun-flints still, from certain remote parts of the world.

Shepherd's book gives the teacher a secure reference background to all this, so that groups can follow up the various topics, with the teacher having a good idea of what to expect.

Use of books

We have said little so far about books and references. A topic can so easily start off well with concrete practical study, then quickly degenerate into second-hand copying of whole phrases (and worse) from books, and frequently the tracing and copying of illustrations, that it is as well to keep reference books out of the way until the children are well advanced in the topic and have amassed a good deal of first-hand information and drawings, and have formed some of their own conclusions. Reference books can then be used for comparisons, and for the extension of ideas. Children need to develop the habit of studying books critically, comparing wherever possible with their first-hand knowledge of the real thing. Part of the planning includes the ordering of County Book Boxes and the like, long in advance of the topic. Bringing in a new local topic each year, planned two terms in advance, enables us to focus our nonfiction library buying on a collection of books covering a specific theme, rather than spread our buying ineffectively over a broad field.

Flint and birds

A topic not mentioned in Shepherd's book excited the interest of two or three of our children. At least two species of birds, one very shy and quiet, the other more common and noisy, lay their eggs among the broken flint and incubate them in an open scrape. The egg camouflage is perfect, and the scrapes are extremely difficult to spot. The first is the stone curlew, one of which we spotted once from a long way away sitting on its eggs only because it opened one huge yellow eye. The other is the nightjar whose eggs, like those of the stone curlew, are just laid in a hollow among the broken flints and fragments of chalk and gravel. Once its territory is known, this bird can be watched and listened to at close quarters, on almost any summer evening. Again, birds like this can be studied at a superficial level of identification and book paraphrasing, but in relation to our topic an important question remains to be asked. Clearly, there is a relationship between the broken flint and gravel, and the colour and shape of the eggs and chicks. Did the eggs adapt in these characteristics to the flint? Did the chicks also adapt? How did these particular birds come to live among the flint? In thinking about these questions, we are already deep into the puzzle of how living things became, in many cases, so perfectly adapted to their environment.

Language

So ancient and important a substance as flint may be expected to have had its influence on language—and indeed it has, in more than one language. Fig. 5.8(a) indicates a few of the words by which a child's vocabulary can be extended. Some, like 'nodule', and 'cortex' are specialist terms. Others, like 'splinter', 'shatter', and 'flake' are more generally used words that should be sufficiently used to make them an everyday part of the child's vocabulary. One of the reasons for choosing a topic should be that it is a ready way of extending the children's *working* vocabulary.

Flint is such a legendary substance that sayings about it have passed into the language. Fig. 5.8(b) indicates just a few of them. Their scope as a starter/stimulus for imaginative writing (and drawing) is considerable. Words and phrases are suggested during the practical work of flint knapping; they are often recorded with the miniature tape recorder, and can be added to or turned into a local studies 'phrasebank' in a card index. As in all topics, the language work arises from the practical activities, but it is deliberately fostered through the teacher's own awareness and the creation of opportunities for using words.

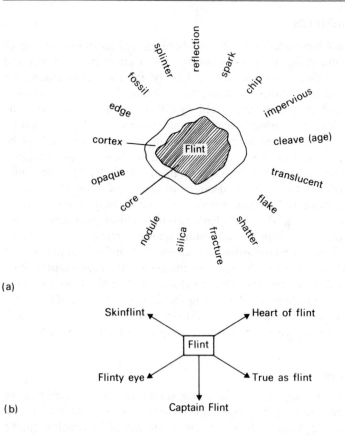

(a)

(b)

Fig. 5.8 (a) Words suggested by a study of flint. (b) Flint: sayings

Concluding the topic

A planned topic such as this one needs to be developed towards some final goal for which a date has been fixed. It needs a satisfying conclusion. Possibilities would include:

1. A specially lengthened assembly to communicate in slides, poetry, drama, for example, what has been learned to the rest of the school.
2. An exhibition, with explanations.
3. A large, composite book of original drawings, writing, photographs, to be kept in the library. The book might be prepared anyway as part of the school's local resources.

Summary

Flint is given as an example of the kind of material that can give rise to a successful, large-scale topic. It is plentiful, full of intrinsic interest, an article of ancient civilization and commerce, and it is local! Many similar materials exist.

The teacher plans the topic over a long period, developing his/her own knowledge with the help of a key-book and references extending from it.

The topic is introduced when the time is ripe, planned over a period, and so arranged that each child completes a core of words (skills or knowledge), and yet has some freedom to follow his or her own interests within the general topic.

Local resources—fields, walls, ruins, buildings, local and county museums, and people—are found and tapped. School collections are built up into something worth keeping permanently. General vocabulary is extended, specialist vocabulary is explored.

Practical investigations are made in depth, and used to develop general ideas from specific properties. Safety in working is emphasized.

The contribution of the specialist, where there is one, is not confined to his or her subject-area. Each member of the teacher-team assumes with the children whatever role the occasion demands. The study works outwards from the flint, its properties and associations, rather than from separate subject considerations focussed on a common object. The components of the study are integrated, rather than combined. The topic becomes a vehicle to stretch as far as possible the children's imaginative and reasoning powers, and their skills.

The topic builds up to a definite climax in which all the teachers and children have had a part.

References

HUXLEY, T. H. (1868) *Lectures and Lay Sermons*, Everyman's Library, Dent, London, 1910.

SALES, R. (ed.) (1980) *Children's Brittanica*, 3rd ed., Encyclopaedia Brittanica International Ltd, London.

SHEPHERD, W. (1972) *Flint. Its Origin, Properties and Uses*, Faber and Faber, London.

Bibliography

BARRY, I. (1980) *Discovering Archaeology*, Longman, Harlow, Essex.

BATES, E. H. and JONES, G. W. (1980) *Elementary Geology*, Shell Education Service.

BURLAND, C. A. (1963) *Fun with Archaeology*, Kay and Ward, London.

HARVEY, A. (1972) *Prehistoric Man*, Hamlyn Pointer Books, Hamlyn, London.

Portesham Environmental Studies Pilot Scheme, booklets available from St Nicholas Primary School, Broadway, Weymouth, Dorset. Booklet 3, *Rocks and Landscapes*, especially applies.

WOOD, E. S. (1963) *Field Guide to Archaeology*, Collins, London.

6. Time to visit the churchyard

Time

Time is a man-made concept which, in the end, merges with distance and space into a dimension which borders on the abstract. You may not agree with this! There is 'useful' time: the hour, the day, the week, even the year. This is time that we can estimate and predict, a dimension we have to use, although diaries, alarm clocks and other devices are necessary to keep us aware of its passing. In practice, even for many adults, most of our ideas of useful time are related to a human lifespan, and, as Piaget and others have shown, the time span a small child can appreciate can be very much less than a year.

We touched on time and sequence very briefly in Chapter 5, and it follows that if appreciation of 'useful' time has such a short span, historical, archaeological, geological, and astronomical time scales have no real meaning at all. It was suggested that, while this might be true of time scales, sequences are a different matter. We can do scale charts of sequences, but in doing so must be aware of the very big transfer necessary for a child to appreciate lapse of time from spaces on a scaled chart.

In the classroom a lot can be done to heighten a child's appreciation of the passage of time; for example, we can make time clocks of various kinds, set up shadow sticks and sundials, chart the movement of sun and moon, keep diaries, grow beans and record their growth daily. With younger children, it may be right that we should stop there; but all too often, even with older children, we neglect to carry this conscious education in time into the further and more distant dimensions, running into millions of years.

The churchyard

A churchyard can provide first-hand material for study of time, of history, and often of philosophy. Most schools have a churchyard within reach of them, and if it is an old and neglected one, so much the better for our purpose. The process of deconsecrating and closing a burial ground is a difficult one, so that even in towns many of them linger on after the population has shifted, and they have ceased to be used. Of course, permission should always be obtained before working in a churchyard.

A churchyard study can be approached from many points of view. Even a well-kept churchyard can be a productive reservoir of wild life; a neglected one can be a positive treasure spot of plants and animals! We have discussed the 'relationship' aspect of wild-life studies at some length in previous chapters; it will not be emphasized here, except incidentally.

The ideas discussed have been developed from work in two churchyards, one unique in that the church was built in Norman times on the site of a bronze age earth circle, rebuilt in the fourteenth century, and ruined early in the eighteenth; and the other an old and quite typical village churchyard. Each site will have its own opportunities, and the topics developed in this chapter can be changed and built upon as the circumstances allow.

Knowlton ruin

The ruined church at Knowlton (Fig. 6.1) and its immediate surroundings are a centre for a truly integrated study. Since all parts of it are visible from anywhere on the mound, simple triangulation and other surveys are possible. Measurements can be taken, heights estimated in several different ways, and the data reduced to scale, according to the age of the children (see further in Chapter 9). The ruined church itself can be similarly surveyed and sketched, and a ground plan produced, from which models can be made. The mathematics involved in such a practical enterprise is considerable.

The tower, much of the nave, and several of the arches remain intact. Leaving aside the lichens and other plants that grow on the stone ruin, a close examination reveals a number of different kinds of stone, besides flint, in its construction. Soft iron and green sandstone may have come out of the river nearby. Limestone must have come from a considerable distance, and we can only guess at the origin of the handmade brick and tiling. A ditch nearby contains all the stone rubbish removed there when the site was cleared and restored by the Ministry of Works. Much of this is flint, but there are small samples of every kind of stone to be found in the ruin. Some of these can be taken back to school, and given the same kind of testing that was described for flint, and added to the school's museum collection. These stones, particularly the flint, the only really local stone, are expressions of geological time. Many millions of years

Fig. 6.1 Knowlton Church ruins

ago they had to be formed from sand and silica, and other substances. Books that help us to identify and date such stones are fairly easy to obtain and use.

An aged yew tree

Round the perimeter of the mounds and ditches are several old, gnarled yews, whose bases are covered in bushy outshoots that conceal rabbit and mouse holes, and piles of oval, olive-green yew berry stones, many of them having a neatly gnawed opening at one end. Two years ago, one of the yew trees fell down in a gale, and in due course, men from the Ministry of Works came to tidy it up. They cut right through the main trunk and left the cut end beautifully exposed. We attempted to estimate the tree's age by counting the annual rings.

The woody cells that carry water grow at different rates and to different sizes in the various seasons, growth ceasing completely in the winter months. When vigorous growth starts again in the spring, a ring is clearly visible. In some trees, the depth of the ring can even say something about the temperature and rainfall in that season. In our ancient yew, the tissues had become very compressed; there were just too many, and they were too close together to count!

Some boys devised a sampling technique; they drew a line across the diameter of the trunk and, using a hand lens, counted the rings that crossed it over a length of one centimetre. This was repeated several times, and the results averaged. Since the trunk was not regular in cross section, several radii were measured, and again, an average taken. Thus, an approximate total for the number of rings crossing a radius was arrived at. The figure was about six hundred.

The children were fairly sure a mistake had been made, but reference to books assured us that yews had been known to live considerably longer than this.

Six hundred years would take us back to the time of Henry V and the Battle of Agincourt, in which we know local archers were prominent. Perhaps their bows were made of local yew. Until it fell our yew tree formed a living link over six centuries. Henry VIII and his wives, the first Queen Elizabeth, and the Armada, James I, and his visits to the local manor, all were yet to come, when this tree was a sapling. Six hundred years ago, too, we could have seen Knowlton Church being rebuilt out of the Norman one. The Black Death had already reduced the working population, sheep would have been taking the place of the former arable farming, and the village of Knowlton and its church would have had about 350 years to go before they became uninhabited, the church ruined, and the village gone.

Looking at the same thing in another way, the carbon, hydrogen, and oxygen atoms that make up the wood in the centre of the yew trunk have been locked up there for all that time, as part of a steadily growing, living system. Now, some of that wood has been taken away to be seasoned, and used for wood carving; some has been burned, releasing those atoms into the air to join in the food cycle again; and the huge main trunk has been left to become a home for many different plants and animals, and slowly to rot. Where the atoms are concerned, time is not relevant. An oxygen atom may undergo ten transformations in two hours; it may be locked up, inert, for centuries, in a yew tree, or for millions of years in a fragment of chalk!

Time-markers

The yew tree, then, forms a direct and living link across a very long period of time (and history). Plenty of other 'time-links' of greater or lesser age are also there to be found. The church building itself spans over 10 centuries, the outer circle and nearby barrow perhaps 35 centuries, and the underlying chalk possibly 130,000,000 years. At the other end of the scale, we can find cowslips with a lifespan of a few years, and common shrews whose life expectation is a matter of months. All of these can be used as a series of markers on a time-scale, for they are all real, and can be seen.

Looking at the two charts in Fig. 6.2, we must be aware that, while the children appreciate the objects as being concrete and demonstrable, the actual proportions of the time-scale pose a difficult abstraction (as all scales do, see Chapter 9). Furthermore, an enquiring child will want to consider the evidence for our statements of age. This leads us directly to how the archaeologist and historian go about evaluating their evidence.

Graffiti on the walls of the ruin are dated, the earliest being in the 1780s, with a steady sprinkling through the nineteenth and early part of the twentieth centuries. The lettering, and weathering, show a steady graduation, making a forged date fairly easy to spot. Such graffiti give pretty definite fixed points on our scale.

The life histories of plants and animals, like the cowslip and the shrew, are obtained by direct observation, and often by marking the individuals, as mentioned in Chapter 3. While it has been shown that a

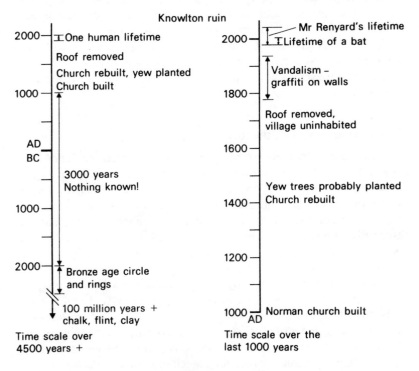

Fig. 6.2 Time sequence charts

common shrew has a life expectancy of less than a year, some of the bats that wheel around the tower each evening have been known to survive for well over twenty years.

The age of the yew tree is again estimated from an observed biological fact, but it is an estimate only. That of the church building is estimated partly from the observed styles of architecture and the materials used, compared with those of other churches dated by independent means. There may also be written records available that suggest, or confirm, the building period of the church (see Chapter 8). Fragments of tombstones, coffin lids, and other objects, worked and sometimes inscribed, provide further evidence, as do pieces of pottery, coins, and other small objects. In making a statement about the age of a church or churchyard, a 'best estimate' is given, considering all the available evidence. In the case of Knowlton, two distinct periods are evident.

Dating the bronze age circle is again a matter of comparison with other such circles, whose evidence is more complete, and of a comparative study of an excavation, and of all the objects found. Very detailed and subtle studies are made, involving excavated levels (frequently thin ones), and often tiny clues buried at the different levels.

We once took part in an excavation of a town centre car-park site, under skilled supervision. The site had been a medieval whelk stall, and we spent a hot day carefully sieving and retrieving all manner of objects. That day, we even established that, at least once, the structure had burned down!

Electronic metal detectors

Visiting a dig in progress can be a very valuable experience. It not only shows at first hand how evidence is put together to estimate ages, functions, and habits, of an age from which writing survives, but it shows very clearly why the indiscriminate use of *electronic detectors* on sites that are, or even may be, important is very unhelpful. The amateur, especially young, detector operator is usually spurred on by motives of personal gain, rather than the painstaking gathering of detailed knowledge. At first sight, the use of detectors would seem to be an exciting and stimulating activity with children. Properly used, say, on the site of a former rubbish dump, it can be, but, as with collecting, it has to be disciplined and diverted away from sensitive areas, where the use of a detector can ruin a site for future archaeologists, to areas where little damage is done. The point is that once objects are removed from their surroundings by haphazard digging, much of their value is lost. It goes without saying that anything like a serious archaeological dig should only be attempted under expert guidance, and with the appropriate permissions.

Dating

Archaeological dating is still largely done by considering the evidence collected over many years for similar sites, and the conclusions drawn. It is done by *comparison*. More precise methods of dating exist, using isotopes such as carbon 14, and those of fluorine. It is said that by their use suitable objects can be dated to within fifty or a hundred years.

Similar methods can be applied to geological samples like our underlying chalk, but again, the age of rock samples is often calculated by comparisons with the order in which other rocks are laid down relative to the one being examined, and the range of fossils found in the rock. Observed facts like the rate of deposition of chalk in the seas, are also collected and used. Comparing the site, its strata, and samples, with the detailed information gained over many years, the chalk deposits may be estimated to be 130 to 150 million years old (see Fig. 6.3).

Just as with all the other studies discussed in this book, it would be possible to make a very pleasant, but superficial study of the Knowlton site, which might include poetry and drama, as well as simple and detailed drawings, and in fact we have done this. It is important, even with the younger children, to take the study a step further into sequence and time, at the risk of their understanding being imperfect, so that they grow up looking for and assessing evidence, and that they experience the real material of history all around them to balance the story-based book-history they started in their first school years.

The village churchyard

The other site is a village churchyard (Fig. 6.4) still very much in use, and containing the recent graves of relatives of some of our children. It has been a burial ground for some five hundred years, the actual grave sites having been used several times at different levels. Again, it would be possible to focus attention on the yew trees, on the wild corners, where many kinds of flowers grow, and even on the fine compost heap in the corner.

At one time, there were rather more wild areas, including some piles of discarded masonry, bricks, and tiles that were rich in slow-worms, beetles, and other livestock. Unfortunately these were all swept away by a working party that came in to tidy up the churchyard. Mercifully this kind of thing does not happen very frequently.

85

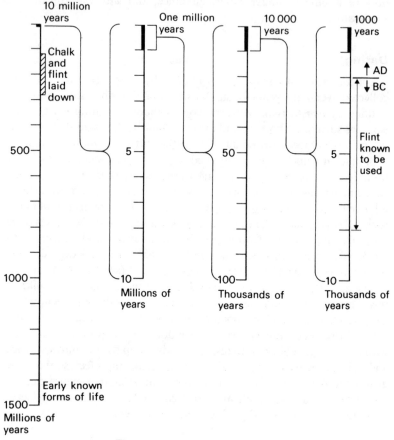

Fig. 6.3 Comparative time-chart

It would be easy to find time-markers in this churchyard, too, and to construct a time-chart. The church dates from about the same time as the one at Knowlton, but this one is still a centre of worship, very much in use, and with complete parish records (see Chapter 8). A thousand years of history waits to be unravelled and put in order.

Much interest centres on the tombstones. The earliest dated ones are from the early 1700s, although there are a number that have been taken up and moved, whose inscriptions have weathered right away. The older lime and sandstone headstones are often heavily encrusted with fine grey lichen, indicating the lack of any pollution in the air; since their surfaces are flat, it is quite easy to measure the growth of the lichen colonies from year to year.

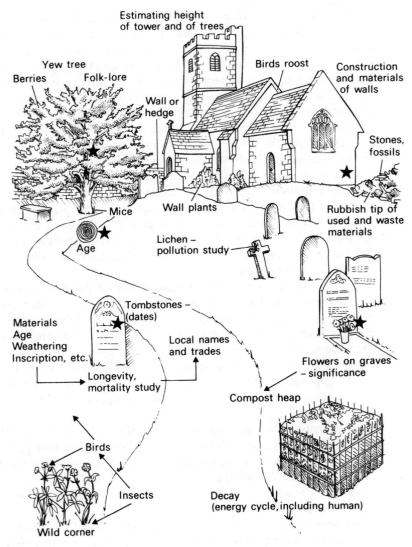

Estimating height
of tower and of trees

Yew tree
Berries   Folk-lore

Wall or
hedge

Birds roost

Construction
and materials
of walls

Stones,
fossils

Mice

Wall plants

Rubbish tip of
used and waste
materials

Age

Lichen –
pollution study

Materials
Age
Weathering
Inscription, etc.

Tombstones –
(dates)

Local names
and trades

Longevity,
mortality study

Flowers on graves
– significance

Compost heap

Birds

Insects

Wild corner

Decay
(energy cycle, including human)

★ Date markers

Fig. 6.4 Aspects of integrated study based on a churchyard

87

Fashion and design of the headstones is interesting, in particular the many ways in which the symbol of the cross has been interpreted. Basically the cross is a strong and simple shape, and it is difficult to believe that it could be developed into so many elaborate shapes and patterns.

The historical value of tombstones lies in the fact that they contain family names and ages, and that they are dated. Details of life expectation at various times can be worked out by collecting ages and dates, and putting them on to charts and graphs. Rubbings and photographs help with the records, too. Two or three stones, grouped side by side, may tell a poignant story, that of continued infant mortality and early death over two or three generations. We suspected, from our dating studies, that life expectation in the mid- to late-eighteenth century was rather better than in the mid-nineteenth, and that life expectation in the mid to latter part of this century increased markedly.

Always against the trend, the tombstones told of some very long lives, in all the periods. In interpreting the readings from tombstones, we must remember that, usually, it was the more affluent whose graves were so marked, and we might expect many of their lives (well-fed and often leisured) would not be typical of the many less fortunate people. A more full and accurate picture is given by a study of the parish records, where these are available (see Chapter 8).

The tombstone study covers a historical span of about two hundred and fifty years. The dates on the stones mean that we can compare their weathering qualities and the effects of exposure in different aspects. Since, in many churchyards, the generations can be followed back from the present day, and often by children who are direct descendants and who bear the same surnames, we have a link between useful time, which can be appreciated ('My granny Smith died last year, and her mother died in 1957'), and historical time ('My great-grandfather lived in Victorian times').

In its function, the churchyard is a place both of time and eternity. The quiet, tidy rural churchyard can be a tranquil place where time goes by slowly. (Reread Hardy's poem in Chapter 1, with time-scales in mind.) The neglected town churchyard can be a place of melancholy and faded memories. Churchyard moods are there to be caught in prose, poetry, and drawings.

We have not yet looked at the other valuable part of the tombstone inscriptions, namely those that tell us what their contemporaries thought of the deceased, and what were their views about the life eternal. Before turning to these fascinating aspects, it is useful to summarize some of the 'prehistorical' and historical skills our children should be practising, remembering to distinguish between experience of time, and a sense of history (i.e., 'What has gone before me, and what, in a sense, is built into me.').

Some prehistorical and historical skills

AGE GROUP 5–8

1. Developing a sense of time in the immediate past.
2. Collecting 'things' (objects) of a period or type, and handling them.
3. Classifying and forming the above into a small, temporary museum.
4. Looking for dates.
5. Making rubbings and drawings.
6. Getting a history 'feel' by going to old castles, ruins, etc., but without much emphasis on time.
7. Watching things grow, grow old, and die.
8. Looking at generations back to grandparents.
9. Short, accurate descriptions, based on facts.
10. All the relevant reference skills.
11. Accounts of feelings, distinguished from facts.
12. Relation as much as possible to time-friezes.

AGE GROUP 9–13

1. Continuation of all points in the younger age group.
2. Local history of one single building or place, collect all the evidence.
3. Display the evidence.
4. Criticize the evidence for probable truth and accuracy.
5. Techniques of surveying, mapping, photography, interviewing (see Chapter 9).
6. Use of local records: library, church, museum, county records, newspapers, retired people (see Chapter 8).
7. All the reference skills.
8. Distinguish the value of forms of evidence.
   (a) Concrete, e.g., flint tools, stones, dates (checks for authenticity).
   (b) First-hand documentary using parish records, etc., letters, tombstone inscriptions.
   (c) Eye-witness accounts.
   (d) Second-hand documentary using sources like public records, county histories.
   (e) Lesser reference books: not referring to original sources, often summarizing other books.
   (f) Children's books, may or may not be factually accurate.

9. Sum up evidence, giving weight to the various forms.

10. Reach conclusions and record them.

We are making the assumption that children will be *doing* history, i.e., collecting evidence at first hand, and coming to conclusions about it; and that side by side they will be learning *about* history from books, films, and other sources.

Much of our history is coloured by stories that have arisen by word of mouth, like those of King Alfred and King Arthur. They have been translated into story books, and embellished over many years. In a child's mind they become mixed up with Bible stories, and those in the more accurate history books, until many children are unable to distinguish myth and legend from fact. By contrast, the people referred to on the tombstones were *real* people, and in making discoveries about them and the way in which they lived we are studying the not-too-distant past in a way that the minds of many children can understand. History books are all selective, as are most newspaper accounts. They can be rewritten (and this happens in many countries) for political and other ends, from time to time. Hence we should be scrupulous in criticizing our own methods and conclusions, and bring up the children with a similar scepticism when they look at history.

It is a useful exercise to go back over the discoveries made at (and the statements made about) Knowlton Church and its grounds, in the light of the checklist given, to see how many of the activities mentioned fit the list, and satisfy the criteria *doing* history, rather than doing *about* history.

Once they have left school, many people never consciously think about the history they studied. It was Henry Ford who said, 'History is bunk!' and, yet, we are all permanently coloured by our understanding of the background of history that goes back to our childhood. It would be encouraging to think that a substantial part of that background included the application of a critical faculty to information gained at first hand, that it would be developed and refined through secondary school, and that it would remain in adulthood as a useful tool.

Some churchyards are heavily populated by marble angels; in others you never see one. Some have elaborate family tombs; in others there is nothing but neat rows of headstones. In some old ones, the stones have all been dug up and placed against the wall, leaving an easily managed greensward, and the message on the older stones has vanished.

The prime function of a churchyard was (and sometimes still is) the burial of the dead in consecrated ground. All around are symbols of life and death. The cross, so often itself a part of memorials and tombstones, tells of a belief in life after death, and in the tenets of the Christian Faith.

Yet we live in an age in which the majority of people have rejected the Christian Faith, and who have grown up in a generation who never go to church except on the three social occasions of baptisms, weddings, and funerals, and, indeed, whose only contact with the Faith was in their teaching at school.

A study of the Christian assumptions made in the tombstone inscriptions is instructive. The words have to be brief, for space is limited. Often there will be a bland statement like 'Peace, perfect peace,' which does not have a particular meaning. Others will refer quite definitely to an after life, and some kind of reunion in Heaven. Such texts occur especially on stones commemorating husbands and wives, and members of the same family.

The earliest stones are often found on the south side of the church, since the north side was usually kept for pauper and other special burials. Almost always, with increasing populations, space became short, and later burials often filled the available ground, which was then used again.

The church and its yard clearly represented such a huge investment of local resources that their faith must have meant very much to the people who built the older churches. The churchyard provides a practical place where teacher and children can consider questions of belief and faith. Many people say that the former widespread Christian belief was a former superstition, which modern people no longer need. This, the philosophical aspect of churchyard study, is not for the younger children, but is entirely relevant for the eleven- to thirteen-year-olds, and can well be tied in with their R.E. lessons.

We have looked at the material and energy cycles, and have seen how there is order and pattern in all we see, for example, in the making of food materials in a green leaf, in their transfer through and use in animals, and in the recycling of materials. We have looked at time, and have found the same orderliness, in the seasons, life histories, and even in the buildings themselves.

Clearly, many people believe in some form or another of life after death, even if they can no longer explain it to themselves.

Many of the time-markers are those of living and dying, such as dates on the tombstones. Our time-chart (Fig. 6.2(a)) has to run backwards and forwards from the date of Christ's birth, such is the influence of Christianity on our time and history.

Primary school teachers will develop this aspect of a general study through R.E. according to the needs of the school. Such work has to be done with great delicacy, since there may be some children who have recently been bereaved. Yet the churchyard and, still more, the church

91

(see Chapter 7) provide a concrete starting point for religious studies, along the following lines. What *did* people believe then? Who *do* people believe now? What do I *believe*? The continuity of Christianity is well shown in an old church and its graveyard. A sensitive teacher may take up strands from the experiences touched on in Chapter 2, and tie them up with different experiences that could arise from churchyard studies, to lead into the spiritual aspects of man's experience.

Very few good books have been written about churchyards and graveyards but the most informative for schools is probably *Graves and Graveyards* (Lindley, 1972). This book is well illustrated, shows what to look for, and gives many ideas for follow-up work.

Summary

It has been suggested that churchyards, graveyards, and church ruins are a good starting point for a study in time. Time-markers are sought for over as long a period as possible—very long in the case discussed of the Knowlton ruin—and in more detail over a shorter period in a conventional churchyard.

To a child, sequence is likely to have more meaning than time, and as much experience of time-charts and sequences should be given as possible. There is a difference between appreciation of time-scales and a study of history. The local time-scales of events, which can be verified, can be tied in and compared with the events of national history, as suggested in the yew tree study.

Children should be encouraged to look critically at the evidence for historical and time-statements, and to consider the ways in which material is dated. Again, books should be consulted rather late in the investigation when first-hand material has been collected and studied.

A local study, such as this one, should go on side by side with acquisition of more general historical knowledge from books, remembering that what is acquired in this way colours most people's knowledge of history for the rest of their lives.

Sensitivity is needed in extending the study from a consideration of man's past spiritual experience, and what it meant to the community, to the state of our present belief, and to a child's personal spiritual experience.

Reference

LINDLEY, K. (1972) *Graves and Graveyards, Local Search Series,* Routledge and Kegan Paul, London.

92

7. Churches and other buildings

Sarah and I went round the church this morning. It was all dark inside, with coloured glass windows. They made a rainbow on one of the pillars. The seats were all fixed in rows, and they had woodworm. There was a funny kind of damp smell, too. At one end there was a big table with a cloth on it. There were two huge candlesticks with candles in, and a big cross in the middle. Sarah said the cross was made of silver, but I think it was aluminium. The arms had big jewels on them . . .

Thus began a ten-year-old's account of her journey of exploration in a local church. For one who could not remember the first time he visited a church, it was a salutary and refreshing experience to wander round one with a child who genuinely had never been in a church before. Her only previously known connection with any faith had been her R.E. lessons in school and at assembly. She had dutifully joined in the 'Dear God . . .' prayers, and she had enjoyed Bible stories from her infant days, without any of it having any impact on any kind of personal or family belief. So she entered a church with no preconceived ideas, no special vocabulary, and very few points of reference. There are many more children in this position than there used to be!

In most long-established communities, the church is usually the oldest and the most substantial building. Much of our own village is Victorian, yet the church foundations date back to 970 or thereabouts. The church represented the centre of village and town life, and not just of worship. Therefore, through the ages, the very best work of architect, stone-mason, carpenter, metal-worker, and glazier has been lavished on it. It represents what is permanent in the community from generation to generation, in design, in execution, in lettering, in fashion, and is at its best when still occupied by a flourishing community to this day. It represents continuity in an age of temporary expedience.

Our environmental study has moved steadily through the chapters from a consideration of the fundamental underlying energy and material cycles in Chapter 1 to a steadily increasing emphasis on the activities of man in the past, which reaches its peak in the present chapter.

Local church visits

There is so much to be explored in, and so much to be learned about, a single old church that it is best treated in the way in which we studied our ditch in Chapter 2. The nearest church may not be the best for our purpose, if it is a comparatively recent one, but we should certainly find the nearest suitable (old) church, and make friends with the Vicar. The teacher needs to get to know the building thoroughly, through repeated visits, becoming familiar with the history, dates, and points of interest. The children are taken on repeated visits, too, preferably in small groups, at first on a general exploratory visit, and then on short visits for special purposes.

Schools vary very much in their association with a local church. There are still many V.A. and V.C. Church Schools that enjoy a close association with their parish church, visiting it regularly, even weekly, for worship, but these are tending to become fewer. Their relationship is a familiar one grounded in *function*. Most children visiting a church do not have this relationship. To them the church is primarily a museum, and it has little to do with real, everyday life. Many of them will not have experienced any kind of corporate worship outside school, and we cannot assume, therefore, that they have any accurate idea of what goes on in the church.

Before we explore the church as a historical repository, we should look at it as a functional place of worship. Its ground plan, its aspect (usually east–west), its furnishings: the Altar, with its candles and cross, pulpit, lectern, font, organ, banners, etc., all have their place in worship. The little girl whose essay started this chapter had no technical vocabulary at all, so we need to start right from the beginning. Ideally, one would start the church study by taking the children to a service; even one specially prepared for the purpose. The church interior is so unlike any other building experienced by the child that it takes time to become familiar with it.

Those early visits are important. Small groups are best, without too much direction. We should not be afraid to sit quietly in the pews, and look and listen.

The sun shining through a stained glass window on to the whitewashed wall, or a thick, cracked pane producing a moving rainbow in a corner is so easily missed. The silence, too, is something that can be felt; stillness is very rarely experienced by modern children. Then there are the smells. The peculiar, damp, musty smell that comes from generations of only being heated on Sundays, is often the prevalent one.

Just sitting quietly, and recording one's feelings and observations is a most valuable early exercise. Alfred Noyes expressed the outcome of this almost exactly in his poem 'The Bee in Church'. The stimulus was a single bumble bee moving through an otherwise silent church on a summer afternoon. Writing from experiences like this can never be forced. It must come from feelings within, struggling for expression.

Some children may prefer to sit and draw, even doodle, while they soak up atmosphere and take in the unfamiliar surroundings. They are getting the idea from the start that they are in a place of worship, a place to which many generations of people have come to spend time in the belief that there is a God who made them and who has an influence on their lives. People in byegone years were baptized in this place, worshipped regularly as children, were married in it, brought their own children to it, and were buried in its churchyard in due course. Tied up in all this is the belief that, far from being an accidental creation on a planet which is itself another accidental creation, man was a carefully planned part of a wonderfully created design, brought about by a creator whom we call God who, furthermore, cares for individuals, and is prepared to receive them after this life, into an eternal Kingdom.

That is what the church stands for, and what the building represents. It follows that, if that is what the people who built the church and worshipped in it all those years believe, they would regard themselves as temporary residents, people in transit to a Kingdom which, as St Paul said, 'Is far better'. Yet each generation did its best to put something permanent into the building, for the glory of God.

It is to be hoped that the children would gain a sense of peace, quiet, and timelessness from their early visits to the church, and some feeling of its function, even if they and their families cannot subscribe to the belief behind it. It has to be said that some of the most peaceful, quiet, and timeless churches are, today, ones that are spiritually dead! I do not say that the children would necessarily experience a sense of worship; but the purely secular feelings they may have are valuable in their personal development and often not gained in any other way.

Church buildings

The older churches of the Church of England (i.e., parish churches) are fairly uniform in their layout. A book such as *Churches* (Pluckrose, 1973) has information at about the right level, and is full of ideas, too. Terms such as nave, aisle, chancel, sanctuary, altar, font, need to become familiar by usage. Many churches have a short guide that gives the basic architectural information and numerous books on church architecture are available. Much of the history of the church building can be deduced from its architecture. The building materials may be local, or they may have come from some considerable distance.

The walls are largely made of flint and sandstone, with later additions in materials of all kinds, including brick. Repairs were often done with the cheapest material that came to hand. If we introduced the idea of time-markers over a large time-scale in the churchyard, those over a shorter scale abound in a church; dates and other clues are plentiful, too.

From the teacher's point of view we could analyse some of them in our own parish church (see Figs 7.1 and 7.2).

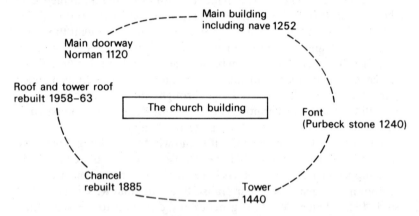

Fig. 7.1 Architectural features (dated periods) as time-markers

These can again be turned into time-scale charts for display, and some of the main historical events of the country superimposed.

The main features of our church neatly cover a period of a thousand years. They can be recorded in detail by drawing, rubbing, and photography. The short bibliography gives a list of books whose illustrations can help children to identify and date what they find. Here, perhaps, is a case where books need to be consulted early a means of identification and the study of function.

Apart from the architecture, other clues to the past are there to be found. Candlesticks on the walls, lectern, and pulpit may indicate how the church was formerly heated, or even just the brackets that formerly held candlesticks may be left. The pulpit may still have an hourglass beside it to time the preacher's sermon. Chests, poor-boxes, leper-slits, coats of arms, gargoyles, these are just a few of the things to be found and looked up in books. In one book (Needham, 1948) we found a section on mural paintings. It is difficult for us to realize that before the

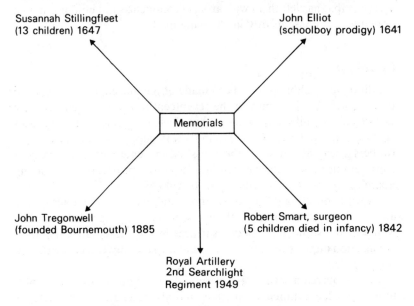

Susannah Stillingfleet
(13 children) 1647

John Elliot
(schoolboy prodigy) 1641

Memorials

John Tregonwell
(founded Bournemouth) 1885

Robert Smart, surgeon
(5 children died in infancy) 1842

Royal Artillery
2nd Searchlight
Regiment 1949

Fig. 7.2 Memorials as time-markers

Reformation, the walls of churches were covered in colourful pictures. The book mentions as favourite subjects, 'The Doom', and 'St Christopher'. We found both of these on the wall of our church. They are thought to date from about 1240, and for many years they had been covered up by layers of lime-wash.

Drawing and painting

Few places provide such an opportunity for drawing and painting as the parish church, yet so many children seem to lack the ability to choose their media and to draw freely. Very young children will draw freely with a fine disregard for perspective and scale. Then comes a period when the anxiety to 'get it right' overcomes all else. The ability to make many lightning field sketches, filling in details and dimensions in words only comes with practice. Like other skills mentioned previously, it has to be learned and confidence gained. Black crayon is often preferable to pencil, with coloured crayons for note-taking. Some of the more abstract shapes, like the flints in the walls, may give confidence because the resulting drawing is obviously neither right nor wrong. Some of the flat shapes, such as memorials and tablets, have an easily copied symmetry. I have seen children guided through a series of drawing

97

exercises that has left them with an easy confidence and boldness in line drawing, and consequently in choosing media.

Rubbings

Traditionally, rubbings have been made of the fine engraved brasses in tombs from the thirteenth to the seventeenth century. Their lines are wonderfully detailed and brass rubbing has even achieved the status of commercial art. The problem lies in its very success, for generations of rubbers eventually destroy the brass! Many churches now charge a considerable fee for rubbing their brasses; others protect them by having fibreglass replicas made, which can be rubbed.

As with collecting (Chapter 3), and metal detectors (Chapter 6), the answer lies in diverting the rubbing habit into less harmful channels. Many of the stone and wooden surfaces in the church are capable of giving good impressions by rubbing, and the rubbings can now easily be photocopied.

We discovered a severe case of vandalism on one of the pillars of a tomb in the local church. A variety of initials, dates and other markings had been carved on the pillars between 1713 and 1938. They were in the dark part of the church, and could easily have been missed. Photography would have been difficult. As shown in Fig. 7.3, rubbing provided a quick record.

Photography

Simple outdoor photography, using a 35 mm camera, can be done by most children. Indoor photography, particularly in the darkness of the average church, involves flash or floodlights. When the teacher proposes to take photographs, the Vicar's permission should always be obtained.

Memorials and social history

Memorial tablets indoors have the advantages over outdoor tombstones in that they remain legible for a longer period, except when let into the floor and walked on; they tend to be earlier in date, and they do not suffer from restrictions in space. They are often informative as contemporary documents, in lettering, style, and content.

Consider this one, erected by a husband in memory of his wife:

> She was a most faithful and loving wife, a religious wife, a virtuous and modest woman during the space of thirty years of her marriage, being the

Fig. 7.3 Rubbings of initials and dates (1713 to 1938) carved casually on tomb column

mother of thirteen children. She was very careful to breed them up in the nurture and fear of the Lord, and to her poor neighbours she was both pitiful and charitable. She patiently and Christianly ended this life, Eighteenth of February, 1647, in the 51st year of her life.

A pious, prudent and virtuous wife.

Note the change in usage of 'pitiful' and the use of 'Christianly' as an adverb. Few men would publicly proclaim the memory of their wives in this way today!

This memorial tablet, from the same period (original in Latin), is to

99

John Elliott, a pupil at the local Grammar School, who is supposed to have died after swallowing a fish bone.

> What a remarkable boy he was!
> Of how great promise, even in early youth. There has scarcely ever been a more extraordinary instance of the powers of memory, of amiability, of intelligence; in a word, all the gifts of nature.
> Whilst striving to improve them by care and study, and, having made an almost supernatural progress, he was taken into the company of the angels.

The verse below is rendered:

> The undegenerate scion of his line,
> NORTON and ELLIOTT in his likeness shine,
> But, seven suns told, all conquering death laid low.
> His parents hopes and him at one fell blow,
> Despotic death that comes with blighting wing,
> To spoil the rich luxuriance of Spring.
> February 2nd, 1641.

What a school report! How old was he?
Some two hundred years later we find a simple memorial:

> Robert Smart Esqr.
> 1771 – 1842
> Surgeon in this town.
> 44 years
> Sarah, his wife,
> died 1867 in her 92nd year
> and five infant children.

Other sources (see Chapter 8) confirm the high rate of infant mortality about this time.

We find a memorial to John Tregonwell (1811 to 1885) who founded the resort of Bournemouth; several to benefactors whose benefaction is recorded in great detail, down to the last penny (and who seem ignorant of, or disobedient to, Matthew Ch.6, V.1–4), and nearer the present time, a memorial to the Second Searchlight Regiment the Royal Artillery, who not only spent part of the war in the village, but whose members kept up a long association with it afterwards.

All these memorials represent people who have worshipped, some from devotion and some from compulsion, over a thousand years. We know the names of all the Abbots, Priors, and Vicars since Giraldus in 1102. For hundreds of years the church was a Catholic one, aglow with colour on walls, furniture, vestments, and windows. We know the exact date when all that began to be changed. It was 31 January 1540 when the Priory was handed over to Henry VIII's men. Since that time, the church has been more plain, stripped out, its medieval murals concealed by layers of lime-wash; that is until one remarkable vicar in the latter part of the nineteenth century carved a chancel screen, a reredos, and tower screen over many years.

Two objects, the font and the pulpit, survived all these changes. Think of the children who have been baptized in that font since about 1240. Think of the sermons that have been preached in the black oaken pulpit since about 1400! Our children read from that same pulpit each year at our Christmas service.

It requires little imagination to populate the church with real people and to write about them. It gives impetus to research about costumes and customs, if the knowledge gained is to be put to use in writing stories about real people who once lived.

This is all part of developing a sense of history by putting people in imagination into real places, and tying them into historical events. We recall Mr Renyard's remark in Chapter 5, about the way he felt when he dug up flagstones that had been knelt on for a thousand years. Stories can be extended into drama, and drama into pageants.

Other churches

Other local buildings may well serve a similar purpose, to provide time-markers, and history-pegs, but few are as readily accessible as the Parish Church. This will not be the only place of worship, however. There will be at least some Nonconformist chapels, and we should extend our study of man's spiritual development locally by visits to these. Methodist and Baptist chapels may be very different internally from the parish church. We touched on the change that came about in the parish church at the time of the Reformation; a further change came about with the Wesley brothers in the eighteenth century and the rise of Methodism, and the development of the Nonconformist movement. In the west of England the Quaker movement led to emigration to the New World. The buildings and memorials of the various chapels record a different tradition of worship from that of the Established Church. Many chapels have now changed their function, becoming private houses and garages. The decline in chapel-going has resulted in many more closures than C. of E. churches, although many of these, too, are being amalgamated and closed.

In many areas, particularly in large towns, it is appropriate to seek out other places of worship, synagogues, mosques, temples and the like, and to look at the beliefs and modes of worship found in other religions. There are two good reasons for this, as part of a study of the local environment. Firstly, it is a continued exploration of the spiritual dimension of man's living, and secondly, we should try to understand the beliefs and customs of our neighbours, in order to live in harmony with them. They, and we, have become part of the same environment. On the other hand, it may not be right to force this in an area in which there are no churches of other faiths, and few people of different beliefs from our own.

Summary

This chapter is a short one, since the study of churches is well documented, and there are many good information books. It is included in a study of the environment because the local church is often made of local materials, is still an important and permanent centre, is a historical repository for the area, and is a natural place in which children can meet the spiritual side of life. They can come into contact with people of past ages whose religious belief permeated their lives and those of the whole community; they can gain in historical feeling and knowledge, and with suitable sequence charts, their appreciation of historical sequence, if not of time, will be further exercised. Hopefully, they can meet people of the present age who profess a living faith, even if they find themselves unable to subscribe to any particular belief. A study of the church in the community shows just how deeply Christianity has penetrated the British way of life, even if to some, today, it is merely a formality and to others, a mockery. The Christian Faith can be seen as providing order and pattern, which we have already perceived in the things around us, extending into the spiritual state.

References

NEEDHAM, A. (1948) *How to Study an Old Church*, Batsford, London.
PLUCKROSE, H. (1973) *Churches, On Location*, Mills and Boon, London.

Bibliography

BETJEMEN, J. (1968) *Pocket Guide to English Parish Churches*, vols 1 and 2, Collins, London.
CALVERT, I. (1971) *Churches in Britain*, Blackwell, Oxford.
MILLARD, J. (1966) *Let's Look at Cathedrals and Churches*, Muller, London.
WARBURTON, C. (1969) *The Study of Churches*, Bodley Head, London.

8. Written records

The Royal Society for the Protection of Birds and other conservation bodies keep a close eye on the killing of all birds and mammals these days, and strict laws have been passed for the protection of many of them. In the Cranborne Churchwardens' Accounts of 1701, we read:

Pd. to John Marlow for 3 doz. and a half of sparrows	7d
Pd. to David Gristo for 2 buzzard heads	4d
Pd. to John Carter for 5 buzzard heads	10d
Pd. to James Shonwood for 9 bullfinches	9d
Pd. to George Hardon for 4 doz. of sparrows, 2 hedgehogs, 1 polecat and 1 stoat's head	1/6d
Pd. to Josiah Gourd for 1 dozen of rooks, 1 dozen of magpies, 6 doz. of sparrows, 4 hedgehogs, 1 Buzzard, 2 Polecats and 3 Stoat's heads	4/2d

The disbursements of bounty for 'vermin' go on for pages (see Fig. 8.1) and indicate, among other things, the very large numbers of birds of prey that existed at this time. We might make a connection between this prodigality of birds of prey and the very large rodent population that could be supported in the poor sanitary and waste disposal conditions of the day. As in the early chapters, we are drawing inferences from what we know today. What was it that buzzards took that caused a bounty of 2d to be placed on each one? Nowhere in the accounts is there any mention of rabbits. We know that both buzzards and kites feed on carrion and small rodents, and it would not be difficult to draw a speculative energy cycle for seventeenth century Cranborne.

Local records

Properly used, local records are among the most fascinating and instructive of our local resources.

The advent of cheap and efficient photocopiers, overhead transparency makers, and 35 mm reflex cameras has made it possible for the school to build up its own collections of local documents so that
1. the most relevant can be selected,
2. they can be studied in detail in the proper place—at school,

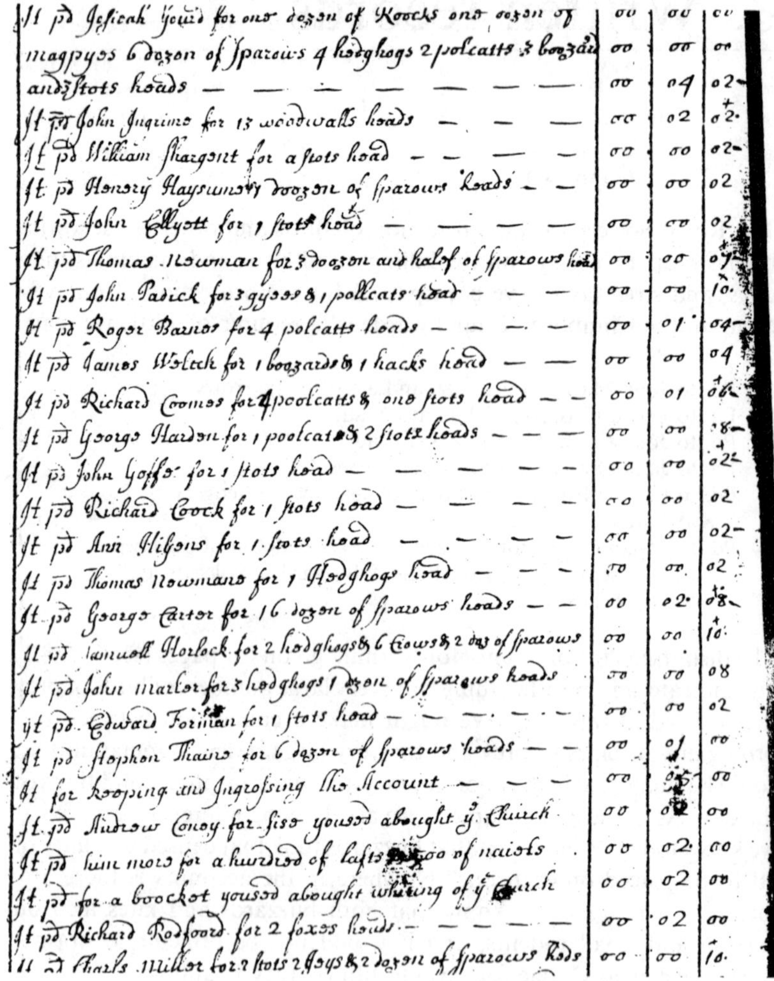

It pd Jesicah Youie for one dozen of Roocks one dozen of	00	00	00
magpyes 6 dozen of sparows 4 hedghogs 2 polcatts 3 bozzards	00	00	00
and 3 stots heads — — — — — — —	00	04	02
It pd John Inquime for 13 woodwalls heads — — —	00	02	02
It pd William Sargent for a stots head — — — —	00	00	02
It pd Henery Haysmere 1 dozen of sparows heads — —	00	00	02
It pd John Ellyott for 1 stots head — — — —	00	00	02
It pd Thomas Newman for 3 dozen and half of sparows heads	00	00	07
It pd John Padick for 3 gyses & 1 pollcats head — — —	00	00	10
It pd Roger Barnes for 4 polcatts heads — — — —	00	01	04
It pd James Welch for 1 bozzards & 1 hacks head — —	00	00	04
It pd Richard Coomes for 4 poolcatts & one stots head — —	00	01	06
It pd George Harden for 1 poolcat & 2 stots heads — — —	00	00	08
It pd John Goffe for 1 stots head — — — — —	00	00	02
It pd Richard Coock for 1 stots head — — — —	00	00	02
It pd Ann Hibons for 1 stots head — — — —	00	00	02
It pd Thomas Newmans for 1 Hedghogs head — — —	00	00	02
It pd George Carter for 16 dozen of sparows heads — —	00	02	08
It pd Samuell Horlock for 2 hedghogs & 6 Crows & 2 doz of sparows	00	00	10
It pd John Marler for 3 hedghogs 1 dozen of sparows heads	00	00	08
It pd Edward Forman for 1 stots head — — — —	00	00	02
It pd Stephen Thaine for 6 dozen of sparows heads — —	00	01	00
It for keeping and Ingrossing the Account — — —	00	05	00
It pd Andrew Coney for fiss yoused about ye Church	00	[illegible]	00
It pd hum more for a hundred of lasts [illegible] of naiels	00	02	00
It pd for a boocket yoused about whiting of ye Church	00	02	00
It pd Richard Redfoord for 2 foxes heads — — — —	00	02	00
It pd Charls Miller for 2 stots 2 Jays & 2 dozen of sparows heads	00	00	10

Fig. 8.1 Churchwardens' accounts of 1701 showing bounty paid for vermin

3. they can be catalogued and stored in school.

Few custodians of written records, unless they are very old or particularly valuable, will object to photocopies being made singly for school purposes. Archives in the care of the County Archivist or some other official body can often be copied at the centre inexpensively.

The church is the most obvious local source for records (see Fig. 8.2). The parish chest will contain registers of births, deaths (burials), and marriages, the Churchwardens' accounts, glebe and tithe maps, agreements and many other documents, although those over 100 years old will often have been deposited in the County Archives, or County Record Office. The local 'elementary' schools could be the next source of information, because log books were kept since their opening. Where the school has been closed, the log books may have been sent to the County Record Office. Farm and business accounts, private houses, and

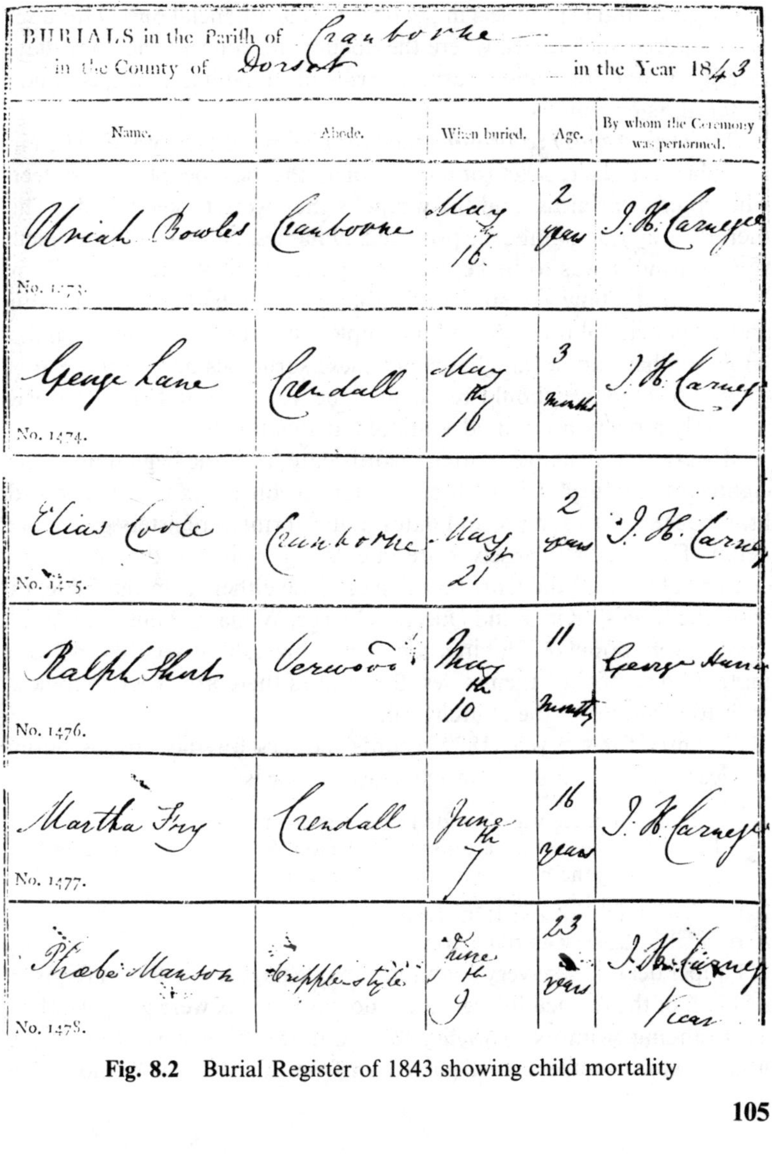

Name.	Abode.	When buried.	Age.	By whom the Ceremony was performed.
Uriah Bowles No. 1473.	Cranborne	May 16.	2 years	J. H. Carnegie
George Lane No. 1474.	Crendall	May the 16	3 months	J. H. Carnegie
Elias Coole No. 1475.	Cranborne	May 21	2 years	J. H. Carnegie
Ralph Short No. 1476.	Verwood	May the 10	11 months	George Han
Martha Fry No. 1477.	Crendall	June 7	16 years	J. H. Carnegie
Phœbe Manson No. 1478.	Cripplestile	June the 9	23 years	J. H. Carnegie Vicar

Fig. 8.2 Burial Register of 1843 showing child mortality

Parish and District Council Offices are other sources of useful documents.

All the above is first-hand material, that is, it is the original document, even if copied in facsimile. National archives often have much older documents, and so do the muniment rooms of great houses. These are not very accessible, except where they are published in volumes such as the Victoria County Histories.

We seal all our photocopies on to standard sized cards, which are catalogued, and kept in sets in the library. The financial outlay for a set of a hundred such cards, where the documents concern the immediate locality, is not great; the return, in terms of individual and class study material, is enormous.

Our earliest study records go back to the time of Henry VIII, when in 1542, he caused a register (or muster) of all the local people over sixteen who could bear arms, and the weapons they were to keep ready. The then Borough of Cranborne provided 29 names. A horse and complete suit of armour was to be kept ready by the town. We read that Thos Welsted had a bow and six arrows, John Shernell had a suit of armour and a helmet, John Golde had a complete harness and a horse; and a large number had nothing! Some of these surnames persist in the area today. Perhaps we should recall that the yew tree at Knowlton was probably already a hundred years old at this time!

Most of our available written records date from the beginning of the eighteenth century. The earliest registers of births and deaths record little but the names, ages, and dates. Later, printed registers give more detail. The names themselves are interesting; well into the nineteenth century almost all the Christian names came either from the Bible, or from the English Kings and Queens. George, William, Anne, and Mary were all very popular. Children can search through the records and gain material like this for themselves. Sometimes there are cross references with tombstones in the churchyard.

An entry for the year 1829 records the fees for the various burial services and gives a social insight into the times:

> A common grave was dug for 1/–, a deeper one 2/–
> To ringing the bell for a respectable person, 5/–, for a pauper, 2/6d.
> For carrying the bier a moderate distance, 1/–
> If more than two miles, 2/–

A beer allowance was paid, too!

Pauper deaths were very common. On one page in the Burial Register of 1792, of the ten deaths registered, no less than six were paupers, their ages ranging from ten to eighty-four. Case-histories exist, too, of the way in which paupers were passed on from one Parish to another in attempts to avoid responsibility for the various Poor Law payments. In several places, the Vicar has signed a deposition that the bodies were buried, according to the law, in woollen shrouds. This was an attempt by Parliament to bolster up the home industry, and was particularly important in our area, which was heavily dependent on sheep.

Through these records, the persons of the Clerk, the Sexton, and the Churchwardens become clear. They were important people, whose functions carried far beyond the church itself.

The Baptismal Registers are of rather more interest, since they list the trade or profession of the father. Fig. 8.3 lists 43 occupations, taken by children from the Baptismal Registers of 1836–46. Allowing for the fact that Cranborne was at that time a market town, and comparably more important than it is today, the list shows how complete was the town's self-sufficiency. Tailor, shoemaker, basket-maker, potter, bridle and bit maker, miller, clockmaker, were all resident and working. All those trades have now gone, for transport is so easy to the bigger towns, and they can no longer be supported. Modern mass production has

Workhouse Governor (1836)	Butcher
Labourer	Draper
Bricklayer	Plumber/Glazier
Cooper	Esquire
Tailor	Chimney Sweeper
Yeoman	Captain of a Trading Ship
Yardsman	Gamekeeper
Blacksmith	Miller
Woodman	Sexton
Bricklayer	Surgeon
Cordwainer	Parish Clerk
Licensed Victualler	Dairyman
Shoemaker	Clockmaker
Gardener	Hawker
Basket-maker	Coachman
Carpenter	Servant
Grocer	Bailiff
Farmer	Relieving Officer
Potter	Innkeeper
Landlord of Fleur de Lys (1837)	Postman (1846)
Schoolmaster (1837)	Officer of Exise
Bridle and Bit Maker	

Notes
1. Most of the entries give 'labourer'
2. Note the wide range of crafts
3. Postman (1846) is early. Cranborne had one of the first post offices in the country
4. There were a fair number of Chimney Sweepers.

Fig. 8.3 Examples of trades and professions of fathers compiled from Baptism Registers dated 1836–46

107

completely altered our way of life. Chimney sweepers were interesting because the next village was the home of the Seventh Earl of Shaftesbury, who played such a large part in getting boy chimney sweeps abolished.The Post Office, too, has a long and unbroken history because of the presence of the Marquess of Salisbury's home in the village. Through these records we find many links with national history, as well as being able to build up a picture of the village as it was in the eighteenth and nineteenth centuries. Two posts in the mid-nineteenth century tell of the grinding poverty that existed in the countryside, those of Workhouse Governor and Relieving Officer. It is interesting with older children to compare our attitude to poverty and being out of work today, when unemployment pay and rent rebates are regarded as a right, with the grudging way in which the Charity and Poor Laws were administered. We have first-hand material to work on side by side with excellent TV and radio series on Victorian times, and, of course, in the later years, we have newspapers, old photographs, programmes, and other similar material made available by local people for copying.

Maps

Maps are another resource well worth exploring. Some very early maps exist of our area, but they are in a private collection, and we were privileged to photograph them. Our best point of reference is the tithe map of 1844, in which most of the tithes of the village were commuted. A tithe is an annual tax paid on each piece of land. Fig. 8.4 shows part of the tithe map illustrating the village and surrounding fields. Our school is built on field no. 215 (shaded) on which the tithe was 2d per year.

This map shows the village and field pattern to have changed very little over the years, a point that was strikingly confirmed by our recent aerial survey. The reasons for this take us into the history and politics of the railways, and provide more first-hand material, for study side by side with the national story as depicted in books in the library. The first ordnance survey map (1 inch to 1 mile) dates from 1811; in black and white, it is full of beautiful intricate hatching and shading. The 6 inches to 1 mile map dates from 1886, although our copy was revised in 1901.

The use of records, especially maps, such as these, must vary from area to area. There are parts of London, Bristol, and many other cities that were villages and green fields not very long ago. Not only do residual buildings exist, e.g., a cluster of old farm buildings in the middle of a modern housing estate, but old maps and records show exactly what the area was like a hundred or two hundred years ago. Where the original settlement has disappeared, the documents may have to be

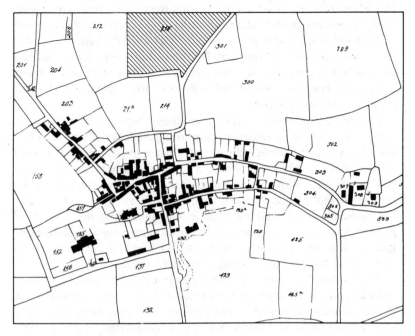

Fig. 8.4   Tithe map of 1844 showing the present school site

traced, but they are usually obtainable if a search is made at the County
Records Office.

Extending the records

In this chapter we have been able to glimpse some of the uses to which
photocopied first-hand records can be put. A whole book waits to be
written on this, and we have so far concentrated on the purely historical
aspect, on building up in the children's minds a picture of the historical
development of their immediate environment, firstly by providing
historical markers and sequences concerned with places and buildings,
and then by the more intimate written material. The use of such material
can clearly be extended by an imaginative teacher far beyond this
immediate use.

Some of the material lends itself to story-writing and drama. In a
neighbouring sea-port town the 'Press-Gang' and other contemporary
stories record the story of a young man, some time before Trafalgar,
who was married at 16 and then promptly press-ganged into the Navy.

This slight story gave rise to a fuller story, then a play, then a play with music, in which a great deal of research had to be done into life at sea on the ships-of-war at that time. Visits to the Victory at Portsmouth, and to Buckler's Hard, where some of Nelson's ships were built, became necessary to gain background knowledge, and in the maritime museum at Buckler's Hard we were actually able to see the original sketches and plans for one of these ships.

The written records of Cranborne Chase include a long series of complicated laws and agreements concerning the Royal Forest. Enough stories abound in court records, and later in newspaper articles to enable a dozen plays to be written. There is a very early authenticated case of a man from the village being hanged for sheep-stealing, and in the eighteenth and nineteenth centuries the battles between forest keepers and poachers have passed into local legend. Smuggling, too, has a long history in the area, and many of the street names, such as Smugglers' Lane, reflect this. Few areas of the British Isles will fail to throw up material of this kind for writing, plays, and songs.

The handwriting of many of the documents can itself pose a problem, as Fig. 8.5 shows. In some cases, the teacher has to carefully make a copy of the wording, adding it to the card in typescript, especially where younger children are using it. A study of handwriting styles is worth doing, especially if the school is interested in italic and other modern derived hands, and at a time when it is the common view that years ago everyone wrote an immaculate and legible copperplate.

Some parish and other records, such as deeds and articles were beautifully written in an educated hand, but many of the clerks who kept the parish registers, and churchwardens, who kept the wardens' accounts, were farmers and people of little formal education whose handwriting was almost illegible. Perhaps we should think of this when we grumble at present-day handwriting, for some of my present pupils, who all write at least reasonably legibly, are directly descended from the people who kept those almost illegible records.

Some children enjoy experimenting with hand and script writing, and our photocopies not only give them interesting material to experiment with and copy, but also to compare with their present writing and with the older formal hands. Numerous books on the history of writing help with the background material.

We should pose the question: What records are kept for posterity today, and in what form are they kept? Churches still keep parish registers in the traditional way; those of births, marriages, and deaths are legal documents. Schools still keep log books. Until now, many people have kept detailed account books. (We saw one recently, where

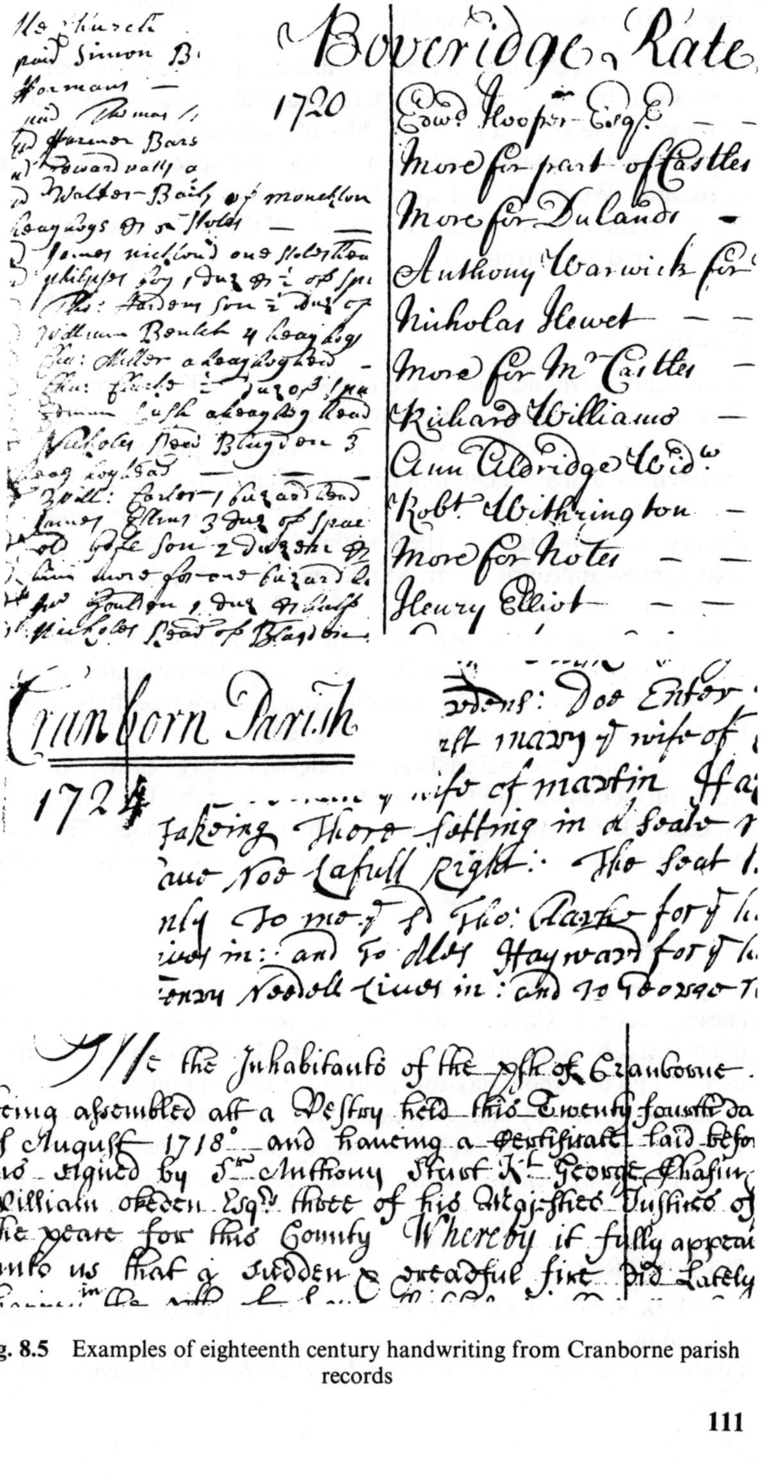

Fig. 8.5 Examples of eighteenth century handwriting from Cranborne parish records

31 years of farm accounts in the early nineteenth century had been kept in one small, bound, pocket book!) It looks as if all this is about to change. Space and time are at a premium. Microfiches, tapes, and floppy discs can store vast quantities of information in a small space, and recall items in seconds. We might well speculate with the children what kind of records of this age they would be looking at if they were at school one or two hundred years from now.

Caution

Many schools will use local materials with which the children have no direct connection, particularly in towns where there is high mobility. In rural areas, and small towns with a stable population there is a considerable danger of children finding out embarrassing details about their not-too-distant forbears. Vicars even late into the nineteenth century did not hesitate to write illegitimate, base-born, or even bastard boldly across appropriate entries in the registers of baptism. A colleague found out some surprising details about his father and uncle while reading a village school log book. Material to be used in school should be thoroughly vetted for suitability; in any case, the original books and papers are too valuable to be brought into school for free study, and the teacher thus has full control over what is used.

For reference, the material can be indexed on large cards. For topic work, further copies can be collated under subjects and put together in Jackdaw-like folders, and a happy combination can be made of detective work with the documents, and background information from books.

Summary

Original records and other historical documents can now be easily and cheaply copied. Church and other sources will provide first-hand documents about the area, especially over the last 250 years. They can be used to find out about day-to-day living in the community at different periods in history, by taking up clues. This can include speculation from what we know already (as in the case of the buzzards). Children are *doing* history as well as reading about it at the same time.

Bibliography

DUNNING, R. (1973) *Local Sources For the Young Historian*, Muller, London.

EMMISON, F. G. (1966) *Archives and Local History*, Methuen, London.

GOURDIE, T. (1981) *The Sheaffer Handwriting and Lettering Book*, published by 'The Sales Machine' for Sheaffer. Has bibliography on handwriting.

The Victoria County History (appropriate County volume), available from county libraries.

WEST, J. (1962) *Village Records*, Macmillan, London.

9. Wheels within wheels

Against the wall of a shed in the corner of one of the fields near school lie the remains of a huge old cart wheel. Clearly visible in winter, with the end of its massive axle, it is almost completely obliterated in summer by bracken and nettles. Its iron rim is still in place.

We have often been to look at the wheel. Once there was a robin's nest behind the hub. As the years go by, weather, fungi, and boring insects are combining gradually to rot and rust it away. Its molecules are subject to the same cyclical processes and transformations as those of the blackberry we found in Chapter 1, the time-scale being rather longer. In a dry, well-ventilated building, timber will keep sound for hundreds of years; neglected in the open, its life is comparatively short.

Our thoughts strayed to the fact that in a Danish peat bog even a ship may be well preserved after hundreds of years, but often all archae-ologists find is a rich mould containing fragments of wood, and a deposit of iron oxide where once the metal lay. It was these thoughts that led us to consider how things rot away, and the conditions under which they do so. As previously when we were thinking scientifically, we sought to set up an experiment in which the variables were reduced to as few as possible. A well-known investigation of rusting iron involves putting shiny nails into tubes and treating them in different ways (see Fig. 9.1). Similarly, pieces of the same wood can be set up, subjected to a number of conditions, and inspected at intervals. Plastics can be investigated in the same way, and it can be shown that they are affected by very few agents of decay.

Our other line of thought concerned the function of the wheel, and the craftsmanship that had gone into it. Apart from building, and then not from the point of view of man the builder, we have not considered in this book man as inventor, innovator, and technologist. Such a theme would need many books to do it justice, but, with the emphasis nowadays very much on saving everything that is old and technological, from farm machinery to the huge beam engines from Cornish mine pumps, no integrated study would be complete without at least a look at this aspect of the environment on our doorstep.

Many topics could be developed, cutting edges, for example, but one that is equally capable of development in town and country is the wheel.

The old cart wheel formed a good starting point, since all its parts were still clearly visible. The hub had obviously been turned on some kind of lathe, bound at the edges with metal, and with twelve sockets chiselled out to take the spokes exactly. The outer rim of the wheel consisted of six parts (elm, we think), closely and exactly joined together to make a perfect circle. Each of these is called a 'felloe', and in each two sockets have been made to take the spokes. The twelve spokes, stout, still faintly red, and perfectly jointed into their sockets, made a completely symmetrical structure. The whole thing is made more complicated by the fact that the wheel is not upright. It staggers outwards, so that the spokes have to be offset. All this the wheelwright would have done by

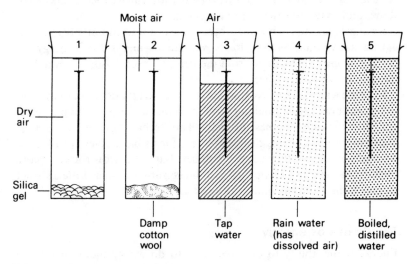

Tubes are airtight, nails suspended on thread

Fig. 9.1 An investigation of the rusting of iron nails

eye. The rim is still tight after all these years. The iron hoop would have been forged by the blacksmith so as just to fit the wooden rim when hot. It would then have been heated in the fire, placed quickly over the wheel and doused with cold water to contract the metal. As the clouds of steam cleared, loud noises would indicate the tightening up of all the joints, leaving the wheel, a rigid, strong structure, ready to be fitted on the cart.

Essentially, the wheel, like all other machines and parts of machines, is a device for enabling work to be done with greater efficiency and less energy than could be done by the human body alone, or with animals. Thus a man can push a cartload on wheels many times heavier than the load he could carry. It can also be used for transmitting energy, and even with quite young children we should be stressing this aspect of technology. Fig. 9.2 gives some idea of the extraordinary richness of the wheel as a topic. Once again, there is scope for practical studies before bookwork. Designing a cart wheel presents technical problems, from the measurement of the circumference to the dimensions and shape of the six parts from which the rim is made. Considerable geometry is introduced. Iron-shod wheels, pneumatic tyres, flanged wheels, fly-wheels, pulley-wheels, water-wheels, windmills, cog-wheels, all can be looked upon as ways of transmitting energy. Not only are the model-making possibilities very considerable, but many kits can be obtained, for example, the Meccano cog-wheel sets with which experiments can be done, and many worthwhile machines invented.

Strangely enough, while the wheel shape is not uncommonly found in nature, its exploitation to lift loads, move loads, and transmit energy has been done entirely by man, from the delicate mechanism of a watch to the solidity of a cart wheel.

Like the wheel, man has exploited the lever to lift and move loads, and to transmit energy for making farm implements for peaceful purposes, and for making engines of war. The technology of the simple manpowered machine is easily explored, for its basic rules are all those we study in elementary science courses, but we discover and explore them from the point of view of usefulness, rather than as little abstract studies done from unconnected work cards.

Man's use of energy

Energy is the ability to do work, and to do work, energy has to be changed from one form into another. We hinted in Chapter 1 at the way in which energy is 'locked up' as food material in green plants, and released as energy to do work in animals, when those food materials are 'burned up' in the process of respiration. Coal and oil are used to fuel a power station, in which heat is produced by burning. This heat in turn produces steam under pressure to turn a turbine in a generator, which produces electrical energy for transmission to the point of use. The electrical energy can be changed into many forms according to need. On the other hand, a fast flowing river or stream will turn a water-wheel, thus providing a constant initial source of power that does not have to be mined or transported. Similarly, wind power has been exploited to grind corn, pump water, and provide energy.

The *Science 5–13 Units, Structures and Forces*, (James, 1973), Stages 1 and 2, and Stage 3, provide the teacher with background information

116

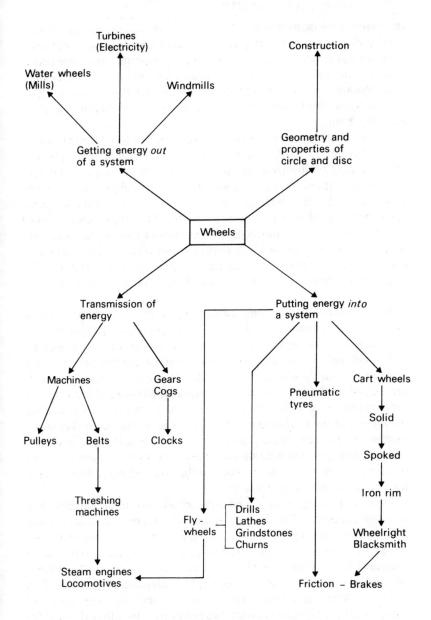

Fig. 9.2 Outline for a topic on wheels. Note that emphasis is on energy input and output throughout

and material for many first-hand investigations, using everyday objects.

With the current popularity of industrial archaeology, and of steam-fairs, vintage fire-engine rallies, and working museums, there are many opportunities for children to see in action the kind of machinery that made Britain rich and famous through the Industrial Revolution. Tape recorders, notebooks, and cameras can be used to record things as they are happening.

Canals, their locks and pumping stations often restored, and railways, where they are in reach, are obvious places to visit. Such visits will undoubtedly have historical and artistic value, and provide rich material for writing—traction engine workings are particularly rich in such experiences—but they will have lost much of their value if the scientific and engineering aspects are not exploited, too. How the machines work, how the energy is transformed, the function of fly-wheels, gears and transmissions, the parts of which were most beautifully wrought in black iron and shining brass, are among the most attractive features for investigation; and many of today's children will happily instruct their teacher.

Almost every area has some industrial history that is worth digging out. We know a number of collectors of old farm machinery, and I once had the salutary experience of having the functions of the parts of an early combine harvester explained to me clearly and accurately by a boy from a remedial class. It may be Bristol, with the influence of Brunel all around, or Ironbridge, in Shropshire, where the history of industry has been turned into a tourist attraction. In a small town in Gloucestershire the history of the world's sheep shears is to be found and in Verwood, Dorset, the pottery industry which spans over hundreds of years has recently been painstakingly studied. Almost everywhere there is a story of man's use of machinery to improve his life and bring him a living waiting to be investigated and recorded.

For centuries, water, wind, and horsepower were all the aids man had in his inventions, and he did a great deal with them. Then came steam, and the industrial revolution. Giant, elegant beam engines and other machines were made, whose technology we can only marvel at in museums today; they seem like great, beautiful dinosaurs! Then came oil, and a prodigal use of an apparently endless supply, and now, in 1982, the wheel has turned full circle. BP and the other great oil companies have closed huge refineries because of the falling demand for oil products. Steam engines are a thing of the past, apart from the steam turbines in our power stations.

The future may be with nuclear fuels, although these are expensive and difficult to harness, and supplies are not inexhaustible, but the search is on to exploit afresh the power of the sun, wind, and water. Solar panels, solar cells, and windmills can be studied on school premises and, again, books on all these subjects are being produced all the time.

Summary

At the conclusion of this small section, which is intended as no more than a glimpse through the window at an important aspect of our environment, these two thoughts may be left with us.

1. Man's ingenuity, which has exploited the earth's resources with elegance, if ruthlessly until now, is quite likely to come up with energy transformations and machines that are only hinted at now. Among our own pupils we have the future inventors and engineers.

2. All man's ingenuity has not yet come anywhere near the economy and elegance with which green plants use a fraction of the sun's radiant energy falling on them, to produce fuel in quantities far more abundant than they ever need themselves. Man has a long way to go, and as the more obvious sources of energy come to an end, his finest engineering achievements may lie in the future in ways we can only dream of now.

References

SCHOOLS COUNCIL (1973) *Science 5–13 Project*, Schools Council/ Macdonald Educational, London. All volumes. *Structures and Forces*, provides a good practical background to an integrated study.

Sources

References and information books on farm implements and machines, traction engines, canals, and other aspects of industrial archaeology published in large numbers. Consult local public library.

The Centre for Alternative Technology, near Machynlleth, Gwynedd, publishes and sells information about and plans for many kinds of home-made windmills and solar installations.

10. Out into the community

When we looked at plant and animal communities in the early chapters we found most of the patterns were concerned with energy and food relationships of one kind or another. In one sense, this is true of relationships in the human community. The resources are limited and they have always been distributed unequally. Until 250 years ago, the population of this country was so low that many village and small town communities could be self-sufficient, or almost so. Inadequate transport facilities made this almost inevitable.

It is significant that only in Chapter 1 have we looked at a community that has not really been influenced by man. The bramble plant will grow in almost any pocket of soil, producing at a given time from very simple raw materials an energy package called a blackberry, which contains the means by which the bramble reproduces itself. This provides food for a number of animals which themselves are fed on by others, so that in a completely wild community a natural balance based on the raw materials and energy available asserts itself. We saw that since our planet is an isolated system within the Universe, whose material resources are limited and whose only outside source of energy is the sun, the same simple rules are bound to apply, in the end, on a global scale.

The ditch in Chapter 2, the walls and hedges in Chapter 4, the flint-based topic in Chapter 5, and the churchyards and church of Chapters 6 and 7, all represent studies of man-controlled communities. As we have seen, human beings are capable of manipulating their environment to a far greater degree than any other organism, and with every generation this capacity grows, until the debate now centres round such topics as genetic engineering, and whether society can spare the resources to allow deformed babies to live. With knowledge goes responsibility, and just as in Chapter 6 it was suggested that children should grow up with the ability to criticize and form their own opinions about what is claimed to be history, and that they should grow up informed about the fundamental energy and material cycles on which our economics is based (scientific thinking, Chapter 1), so they should grow up with a knowledge of communities and the interrelations between them. In this chapter we explore the route that leads out from the school into the local community, since that is another concrete resource with which the children can become familiar.

Maps and surveys

MAPPING

One of the basic tools for this study is the map. The development of the mapping skills is too often taken for granted, like the development of a child's concept of time. A map is a very abstract construction. Reading one involves transferring information from a two-dimensional symbolic picture, on a much reduced scale, to a three-dimensional actual scene that may stretch to the horizon. Making one involves the reverse process, of representing a large, three-dimensional scene, on paper, in symbols, on a reduced scale. Just as we teach children to read and write in steps, so they should learn to interpret and construct maps and, indeed, graphs and other pictorial representations by stages. Until they can do this on a very local, concrete scale, there is little likelihood of their appreciating the larger and more complicated maps to be found in atlases.

A list of skills to be drawn on in the making and reading of maps, chiefly mathematical, might be as follows:

1. Appreciation of distances (measured and estimated).
2. Space (area): regular and irregular, and its measurement.
3. Shapes: regular and irregular.
4. Pictures, charts, and plans of simple objects from life.
5. Pictures, charts, and plans from memory.
6. Three dimensions represented in two simple plans.
7. Collecting numerical data.
8. Collecting/classifying objects and pictures.
9. Reduction scales (a high order skill).
10. Orientation: left, right, points of compass. Use of compass.
11. Symbols to represent objects.
12. Coordinates.

Harris (1972) gives an excellent approach to the early mapping skills.

Fig. 10.1 indicates one possible step-by-step approach to the making and reading of a local map. Simplified maps of the area can be made by the teacher, tailored to a particular purpose, and to the children's stage of development. The Banda is the traditional way of reproducing such material, but the overhead projection transparency, with the ease of adding overlays and adding and rubbing out information, is a powerful tool which is not always fully used.

Like other maps, home-made ones for specific purposes can be made more permanent (Roneo or, better, offset-litho at the Teachers' Centre) and sealed on plywood boards with plastic. They can then be drawn over with crayon and wax pencil, and rubbed out again with a duster, and, of course, used from year to year.

121

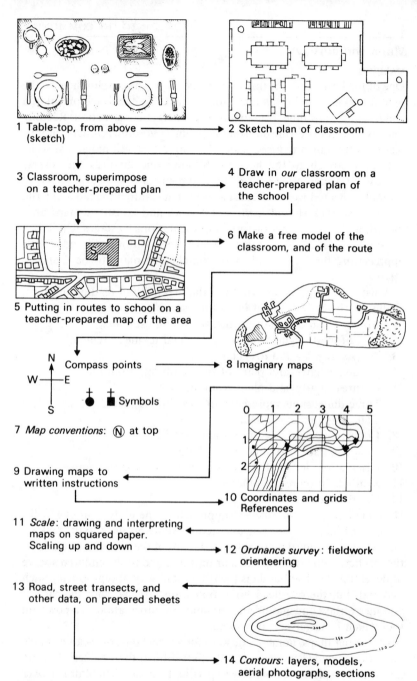

1 Table-top, from above (sketch) → 2 Sketch plan of classroom

3 Classroom, superimpose on a teacher-prepared plan → 4 Draw in *our* classroom on a teacher-prepared plan of the school

6 Make a free model of the classroom, and of the route

5 Putting in routes to school on a teacher-prepared map of the area

N
W—E
S
Compass points → 8 Imaginary maps

7 *Map conventions*: Ⓝ at top
Symbols

9 Drawing maps to written instructions

10 Coordinates and grids References

11 *Scale*: drawing and interpreting maps on squared paper. Scaling up and down → 12 *Ordnance survey*: fieldwork orienteering

13 Road, street transects, and other data, on prepared sheets

14 *Contours*: layers, models, aerial photographs, sections

Fig. 10.1 Outline of a step-by-step scheme for the introduction of the main mapping skills

Early mapping studies will probably be based on the school and its grounds, and on the route by which the children come to school. In a city school, routes to school will often be concentrated into a mile round the school, occasionally very much less. An area school may involve ten or more villages stretching up to ten miles in each direction, and most of the children will come to school by bus. The principle is the same; to use the information provided by the children to the full, since this does not involve going out of school and wasting time in travelling. Fig. 10.2 shows a direction and distance chart (originally done on squared paper)

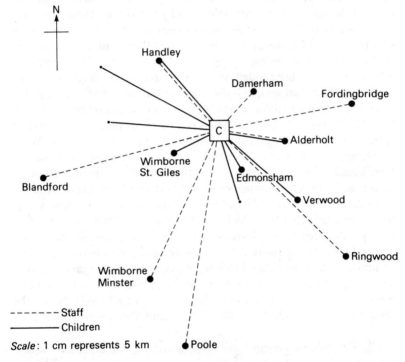

Fig. 10.2   Direction and distance chart showing home areas of children and staff (numbers could be added)

comparing the direction from which children come, and from which the staff come, in a rural school. The same could be done in a town school, but the scale of travelling would be smaller.

SURVEYS

The other basic tool for studying people in their environment is the survey or census, and the associated technique of sampling. Its development goes side by side with that of mapping. Comparisons of heights, colour of hair and eyes, collection of information about teeth, collection of the information to construct the chart (Fig. 10.2), all involve the identification of precisely what we want to know, and a formal way of asking the questions and recording the answers. Early surveys will involve a whole population. Again we can use all the facilities of the school to gain a great deal of information in a short time. In our school, dental information concerning the origin of tooth damage was gained very rapidly from 500 children. The survey provided actual data to work upon, and the results and conclusions were of interest beyond the school; they were taken up by the Dental Health Service.

The point is that the children can learn the techniques of survey construction, administration, and the handling, interpretation, and display of data without ever going outside the school to do it. Sampling, where a school is big enough, can be introduced and developed in the same way. The ideal sample is the whole population. As I write this, the largest whole population survey we ever take is going on all around me—the National Census of 1981—but for most purposes we have to extrapolate from a convenient sample in our interpretation. What represents a convenient sample? What size of sample is statistically significant? This leads us into averages, and the mathematics of statistics. As in science, much of what has traditionally been left to the secondary school may well be introduced in a simpler, concrete way with much younger children. Pocket calculators are tools we use with younger children with reluctance, although many already have their own at home, and in the next few years we shall certainly see the micro-computer, and its associated techniques, coming into the junior school. The new generation of children are *not* just going to need to read and write. They will need to interpret information of all kinds; hence, the need to introduce the map, the survey, and the sample as early as possible.

Like the collecting instinct, the metal detectors, and other techniques, the *survey*, once it gets outside school, can easily get out of hand! In any popular Dorset town or village near a school study centre, you will find young people (with clip-boards) politely stopping people in the street, or going from door to door asking for answers to questions. The trouble is that many of the respondents are weary of answering the same or similar questions so frequently. A house to house survey needs Police permission, and some surveys cause considerable annoyance because they use the same area more than once, each group being ignorant of what has gone before.

The answer is not to stop doing surveys, but to prepare the ground thoroughly, by asking permission to do a survey in a limited area, and stating exactly what will be required, and when the survey is to be done. The questions need to be prepared thoroughly, so that the answers will really give the information required, and that the actual questions do not give offence.

Harris (1972) goes into detail on the subject of making map or symbolic surveys as opposed to the social surveys mentioned above. Starting with a simple transect (literally, collecting all the information that touches a line, laid down actually or in imagination) along a hedgerow or in a park, it moves on to a road transect in a built-up area, and then a street profile that codifies information about shops, trade, and services (see Figs 10.3 and 10.4).

Gathering information in this way can be done in the immediate neighbourhood of all schools, and full use should be made of all the local possibilities before moving further afield to gather information in a similar way.

Contours, the representation of height on a two-dimensional figure,

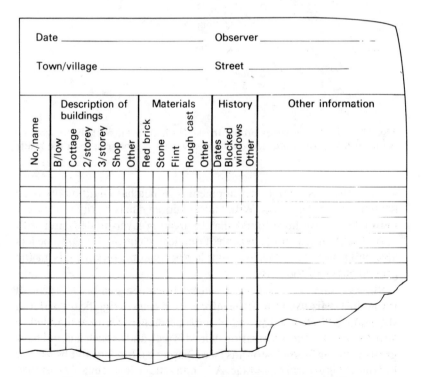

Fig. 10.3 One of many ways of recording a street profile

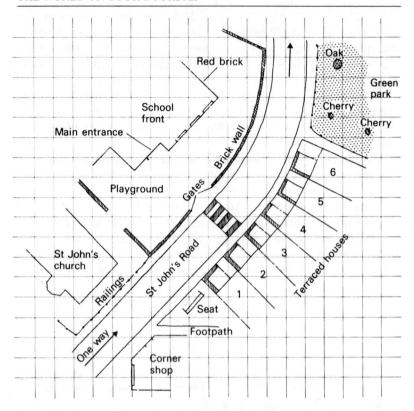

Fig. 10.4 Part of a street profile in sketch-map form, roughly to scale on squared paper. (A *transect*, recording only what can be seen from the road)

are a further abstraction, development of which has traditionally been left to the secondary stage. With many children it may be right to leave it until late, but we have found that by making layer-models, and with partial help, such as the provision of duplicated cut-outs, even some less able children have come to a simple appreciation of contours in the general shape of the map.

Surveys, sampling, and maps will be developed steadily all through the middle years. As with all the information gained, significant material should be collected and stored in some permanent form, and added to year by year, for the information gained is real, and as such it could have great value for future historians (see Chapter 8). Folders and books are but one (bulky) form of storage. A 35 mm reflex camera enables detailed pages to be stored on 5 cm^2 transparencies, and in the very near future it will become easy to make prints from these, when required (it is possible at present, but expensive). We should be forward-looking in our storage as well as in our techniques.

The gathering and interpretation of physical data is important, especially since houses are pulled down, woods felled, and hedges uprooted. From year to year, similar studies can be made and surveys conducted to build up a collection of material from which trends can be seen.

The 35 mm camera provides a rapid way of recording what is seen, but, as with the churchyard and the church, children should still be encouraged to gain confidence in sketching in a variety of media. In this way they can provide working drawings, annotated, from which drawings can later be worked up in more detail, including, of course, composite pictures and collages (see Fig. 10.5).

We must not forget that a community consists of people, not places, and the emphasis should be on the interaction of people in the community. The basic geographical techniques of mapping and survey work are concerned with the gathering and interpretation of data. Coming into contact with people in the community involves looking at the available resources.

1. *Parents.* This is the most numerous resource, comprising shop-keepers, firemen, bank managers, garage owners, farmers, nurses, etc. Find out which of them live in the area, and what could be gained if they came to school, or we went out to them.
2. *Services.* Police, Fire, Ambulance, Postal, Electricity, Water, Gas, etc. What contacts do we have? Which could be followed up and lead to visits?
3. *Local Government.* Parish, district, county councillors and officials, magistrates, probation officers, social workers.
4. *Churches.* There may be more than one denomination/religion, for instance, is there a Rabbi?
5. *People we can help.* Old people (at home and in care), and young children (playgroups, nurseries, children's home).

Interviewing and recording

Mention has been made at various points in this book of local people who have helped our school enormously, and have enjoyed doing it. The teacher can arrange for adults to be interviewed, either at their home or at school. Such interviews, especially where the children learn the technique, and use small, non-threat tape-recorders with confidence, are an extremely valuable extension of language work. As with survey techniques, the children can practise on themselves before going outside the school. They can learn how to put people at ease, how to gain positive responses rather than 'yes' or 'no', and how to structure an interview so as to gain the information they want. The resulting material can often be used in assemblies. Recent child-to-child interviews in our school have involved lace-making, lambing-time, renovating old motor bikes, bell-ringing, and a flight in a light aircraft. Only when the children are confident, and neither tongue-tied nor careless, should they be let loose on adults outside the school.

Elderly people and colourful characters (who need to be sought out and warned beforehand) often appreciate being visited at home, especially when cakes made at school accompany the visit. Stories, opinions, things from the past are all grist to the mill, but the children should be able to obtain specific information when this is required. For example, as part of a topic on water and its supply, we discovered that mains water only came to the area in the late 1930s. How did people get their water before then? We reasoned that there must be plenty of people who could remember long before then, and the interviews not only gave us information about springs, wells, dew ponds, and storage tanks, but also what it felt like to carry water, not just for domestic use, but out to the farm animals, sometimes having to break the ice first.

The lives of individuals and of families is important; so is the way in which they work together as a community, and the way in which they care (or do not care) for each other. A local study should include the rules and the way in which law and order are maintained in the community. Here again, we can start within the school, looking at the need for rules in school, at privileges and responsibilities, at where the resources come from to run the school, at the authority structure, and at the quality of individual lives that results. What is freedom? Can you have it unless there are bounds?

Of course, the basic unit that should be studied is the family, but few teachers could take for granted that all the children in any one class all came from stable homes, two parents, and regular marriage unions. We have to find new ways of looking at the family in school—ways that will support the basic pattern of the family, without hurting the many children who are being brought up outside the traditional family unit. Unlike the material/energy patterns in our blackberry, or the seasoned pattern of bud–flower–fruit–seed by which the bramble is produced and maintained, human social patterns are in a state of very rapid change. Many of us felt at one time that social education was not the school's job. It seems that we cannot escape it now, even if we wanted to.

Having thoroughly exhausted the resources of the school's social environment, we can go outside to look at the social services in the community. Younger children will look at the Police, Fire, and Hospital services, as they have done for many years, but perhaps with a change of emphasis. Who pays for them? How are they paid for?

Older children may look more closely than before at the authority structure in their school and home area. This is a very sensitive field of study, even with younger children, since attitudes to authority, including the Police, have changed, too. We can gather information in an objective way—but how far—and how should *we* as teachers influence attitudes? These questions open up big issues and go along as yet uncharted ways. They are political.

Community projects

Finally, the school can take part with the neighbourhood in some combined project. It may be the turning of a derelict corner into a garden for blind people, in which the children have to consider an environment in which one vital means of gathering information, that is, sight, is missing. It might be a regular programme of visits and entertainment to an old people's home. Whatever it is, it must involve the children in real, not contrived cooperation with adults outside the school. The collection of acorns for a tree nursery once led a school to care for a growing plot of oak trees in a nearby forest. The restoration of a pond and marshy area led to the eventual building of a bird hide. Nesting boxes have been put up outside hospital windows. In most cases, what started as a 'one-off' project turned out to be a lasting commitment that not only helped the children to learn, but contributed to an improvement in the quality of the living environment.

The immediate school environment, even when it consists of unbroken rows of houses in dull conformity, can still be a rich source of inspiration for writing, drawing, painting and three-dimensional work. If you send the children out to sketch they may well say, on the first few occasions, 'I can't find anything to draw'. Properly conditioned into seeing, and given freedom to use a variety of media and make mistakes, they will come back with sketches of backyard dustbins (and cats on them), lines of washing, kerbside drains, lamp posts and other patterned objects that an adult would never think of. Put together as a collage, the material gleaned from one ordinary street, with some short, vivid words of description can be a valuable record of freely gained social information that should find a place in the permanent collection.

Just occasionally, this line of work can lead to a kind of abstraction that is based on the summing up and digestion of a lot of information.

129

Fig. 10.5 is a photograph of a piece of ceramic, rich in browns and creams in the original, matched to a fabric background that gained its inspiration from a view of our village. The church, the Manor, the houses, all are there, twisted and turned, but in the finished result, unmistakably our village. It was made by a twelve-year-old.

Fig. 10.5 Abstract of the village in ceramic and fabric

Taking part in local events can spill over into environmental study, too. One year, a class decided to make a Christmas card for the village, to be illuminated by spotlight, in a dark part of the Church. The eventual product, made by 30 children, measured eight feet by four, and stood on two easels. The story was simple: 'If Jesus were to be born in these days, and Mary and Joseph were going on a journey, being poor, they would be travelling in an old car. Supposing it broke down in Cranborne Square . . . . There is a shed behind The Sheaf of Arrows. They could go there . . .'. Not only the shepherds, but the sheep, dozens of them, came down from the hills to pay homage, together with the nurse (who might be needed), the Vicar, the postman, and even the Head of the Middle School with a crocodile of children bearing gifts. A helicopter (news media!) hovered overhead.

In the giant collage, the buildings of the square, the church, the Manor and the trees were authentic. The Lowry-like figures told the highly original story as the collage developed. A piece of imaginative writing and artwork was naturally and genuinely developed from a fairly prosaic and concrete study of the village architecture.

1980 was Millenium Year. The village celebrated a thousand years of worship in the Parish Church with a whole series of events. We researched and developed two fabric collages. The first, made by older girls, their teacher, and helped by a number of local people especially in the research, depicted, in detail as faithful as possible, seven scenes in the history of the village, from the Norman Motte to the opening of our school. This was a highly sophisticated study involving detailed drawings of all the buildings involved, and intensive work from contemporary sources like photographs.

The second (Fig. 10.6) was a more free interpretation by younger children of the village as it was in medieval times, when the river ran through the street as an open brook. The research was more general but, again, a group of children produced something that was undoubtedly a work of art from a study of their local environment.

I thought we were particularly favoured in the richness and possibilities of our particular environment until, visiting a big industrial town in the North recently, I came across in a middle school a most wonderful interpretation in greys and browns, of the mills and people

Fig. 10.6   Part of felt collage: the village in medieval times

round that school, using exactly the same techniques as we had used for our village scene. In both cases, the research had been thorough, the background authentic, and the interpretation free.

Summary

In this chapter we have explored the school as part of the human community that it serves. We have only glimpsed in passing at all the human relationships that are there to be studied, and we have seen how easily an objective study can become a social study, and how this can lead to political considerations. We posed the question as to whether the school should influence children's attitudes, or whether it can avoid doing so, if its children and teachers become involved in the lives of the community.

It is important that we should give the children the fundamental skills of map-making and interpretation, surveying, and sampling, so that they may know how the information they see in newspapers and on television is gained *and used*. They need a critical appreciation of the conclusions put before them.

Modern needs and modern methods may well mean that the early skills should be started in the junior school. Tape recorders, calculators, and micro-computers will be a natural part of our children's lives as they grow up. We can assimilate them and learn to use them in our environmental studies.

The school needs to become involved with the local community as part of its study of the environment, with a two-way flow of people in and children out, sensitive to the changing needs of individuals and the changing social pattern. In all of this we should see moving patterns, and the opportunity should not be missed of turning them into writing and art forms of all kinds.

Perhaps above all, we should be concerned to demonstrate right from the start, a care for the quality of living of individuals and the community, and a determination to improve it when we can. The concern starts within the school community and the school environment.

Reference

HARRIS, M. (1972) *Starting from Maps, Schools Council Environmental Studies Project*, Hart-Davis, London. Supporting material in *Teachers Guide* and *Case Studies* in same series. *Teacher's Guide* has full bibliography.

11. Aerosols and bottle banks

The denuded ditch

We went back to the ditch last week, for the first time this year. All those trees, including blackthorn and ash, and the festoons of clematis, had gone; they had been cut down to the ground and burned, leaving just the bare slopes dotted with stumps. Only time will tell what will happen to the orchids.

It is difficult to explain to the children why they should pick no living thing, yet the tractors and chain saws can come in and clear everything out in next to no time. How do you explain something like this to children who have been brought up to think about energy and material cycles, and balances?

On the way out, near the car park, we stopped to look into a rubbish bin. A sad sight met us there, too. On top of the rubbish, and covered with a carelessly discarded cigarette packet, lay a freshly shot young rabbit, once a wonderfully put together combination of atoms and molecules that was warm and moved, and responded to the stimuli around it. In the terms of the energy cycle outlined in Chapter 1, one could have understood it if the rabbit had been shot for food, but here the fun came in the shooting and the body was discarded. How do you explain that to children who have been brought up to respect living organisms, and to believe that all of them have their place in the pattern of creation?

Future archaeology

Sitting on the bank, another thought came to us. Supposing we were archaeologists in a thousand years' time excavating the ditch and mound, what would we be likely to find in the way of objects left by this generation, and what would we make of them? The children dispersed to see what they could find and returned with the following items:

A dozen shiny rings that would fit a finger.
Three plastic vessels with intricate blue crosses on the outside.
A torn sheet of transparent material.
A red object pointed at one end and flattened at the other, rather like a soft, flat nail.

None of these things, we thought, would be likely to decay over the years, provided they were under the soil. But what would our archaeologist of the future make of them?

The rings might well have been ornaments, or even wedding rings, for it was well known that people still got married in those days and exchanged rings. But there were rather a lot of them. (They were of course, soft-drink can tops.) The plastic vessels may well have had some religious purposes; for it was known that in those days the cross, in its various forms, was a popular religious symbol. (They were, in fact, ice-cream cartons.) The transparent plastic could have been part of some kind of window. It excited little interest. The final object, the red, fat, flattened-headed nail, finally had to be labelled 'function unknown'. It might possibly have been part of some kind of fastening. (Actually, it was a golf tee.)

The lesson to be learned from our musings is that after a long period of years, archaeologists *may* come to quite the wrong conclusions about some of the things they find. They reach their conclusions on the best *evidence* available to them. Our archaeologist of the future will probably have an inheritance of pictures, slides, film, video-tape, with a vast quantity of information, such as does not now exist for any time in the past. Knowledge is increasing, and being stored in an organized way, all the time. What have we added to that knowledge from our school studies? Have we reached our archaeological and historical conclusions by considering the best evidence available?

Now that the ditch has been cleared and cleaned out, our very detailed set of slides has a double value. They record what *was* there. They cannot be repeated.

Aerosols

Not long ago, we read an article in a magazine about the dangers of using aerosol cans. A survey of our homes revealed that a class of 31 children found at home a total of 510 cans, covering 24 different products, an average of 17 cans per household. They ranged from touch-up paint and furniture polish to body spray and oven cleaner. We thought briefly about the cost of all these cans, for they all had strong concave bases, and strongly seamed sides. They were, after all, pressure cans. We explored some new words like diffusion and dispersant. Apart from the danger of fire and explosion, we read that the dispersant from all the millions of aerosols shot off into the atmosphere was actually causing atmospheric changes. It apparently attacks the ozone in the ozone layer, changing it into something else. The ozone layer in the atmosphere filters out a lot of the rays, including ultraviolet rays, that would otherwise penetrate to the earth, and possibly harm our bodies. At the moment, these rays do not normally reach a concentration that would do our bodies harm. But, it is said, if the ozone layer is being constantly attacked by the dispersant gas, it will thin out, and, in time, the dangerous rays *will* penetrate to the earth.

That is what the article said. Some of our eleven-year-olds tackled this critically, finding out all they could about aerosols, ozone, and the atmosphere. They recalled what had been said some time before when we were studying what happens when coal and oil are burned. Large quantities of carbon monoxide and carbon dioxide are produced. Millions of years' worth of coal and oil are being burned off in less than two hundred years. Could that increase the percentage of carbon dioxide, and decrease the oxygen, in the atmosphere? And would the fact that the established green plants (from hedgerows to tropical rain forests) are being cleared away tip the balance still further, by not using up the carbon dioxide at a fast enough rate?

The possible ozone reduction was the same kind of problem. We did not come to a 'right' answer, but we concluded, on balance, that the effect of all the aerosol cans put together on a vast reservoir of the earth's atmosphere was not likely to have a great effect. The children were able to transfer their thinking from the coal/photosynthesis/carbon dioxide cycle to the new one of the ozone, find out the (limited) evidence that was available to them, and come to a reasoned conclusion. Very few indeed of our pupils will become professional scientists, but the more able, whatever they eventually specialize in, ought to have the tools to look critically at what is put before them by governments, the media, and other interested parties.

Thinking further about the ozone layer, and the possible effect of dispersants leads us to think of the large-scale crop spraying that goes on in our area, much of it from the air, the jettisoning of fuel at airports by aircraft landing, and the fumes produced by their engines, the effect of thousands of tons of rocket fuel burning off as space shuttles and satellites are hurled into orbit. This is just a glimpse at the way man is modifying his environment.

The bottle bank

Lest it be thought that this book, having taken us through moments of tranquillity and times of inspiration, should end on a despairing note, there are hopeful signs. Listed recently among the attractions of Salisbury was its bottle bank. Apparently, people bring their used bottles from a considerable distance to hurl them with a satisfying crash into the containers below. The shattered glass is reclaimed as cullet, which will be recycled as part of the new glass to be used again. Glass is mostly silica, flint is composed of silica, and flint is one of the most durable substances known. From this small beginning there may come a recycling programme for all the other valuable materials that our profligate society uses once and throws away.

Summary

Notwithstanding our disappointment at the ditch, and our dismay over the rabbit, there *is* a value in bringing up children from their very early days to know the patterns that are fundamental and unchanging. They have all appeared at some point in this book and they may be summarized.

MATTER

Matter is made up of tiny particles (atoms) of a comparatively small number of kinds (elements), joined together in groups (molecules). Molecules are constantly forming and reforming so that the atoms move from substance to substance. Always there is movement.

ENERGY

The movement mentioned above requires energy. Some combinations give it off, some use if up; often it is stored. The only external source of energy is the sun. Green plants can store it in food materials. It is released by burning (in living things, this is respiration).

All growth, movement, change, reproduction, requires energy.

CHANGE

A few things, such as chalk and flint, stay stable and unchanged for millions of years. *All* change in the end into other substances. Things are being built up and broken down.

SEASONAL CYCLES

These cycles depend on the sun's energy. The reproduction and growth of many plants and animals goes in seasonal cycles.

RESOURCES

These are limited. They may be locked up for millions of years; they may be made and used in a day.

Man uses resources more quickly than they become available. The history (and pre-history) of man's use of resources can be studied by the clues left in each period.

MAN'S RELATIONSHIPS

In his communities, man's relationships are greatly influenced by the resources available to him and how they are shared. He cannot (yet) go outside the natural rules (or laws) that govern this planet. Man alone can modify his environment.

Man reaches into a spiritual environment as well as his material one. Stonehenge is one expression of this. Our village church is another.

Man is capable of creating and remembering such things as thoughts, words, patterns, music and pictures, and is immensely rich in being able to do so.

Probably every age has appeared unstable and full of change, and even threatening, to those who lived through it. Certainly the pace of change can never have been greater than it is now. The stable threads, of

Fig. 11.1 A dandelion parachute, magnified

energy, of time, of space, that underpin it all, can be teased out of the complicated pattern that forms the school environment.

Have you ever blown dandelion parachutes from a ripe dandelion head? Did you notice how they flew, their direction, the distance covered? Did you see what happened when they landed? If you put one under a good lens you will see a group of beautifully sculptured, outward curving spikes on the stone. It did not stay where it dropped by accident!

Index